CONTENTS

INTRODUCTION

Five miles from my front door in Leeds there is a gentle valley, mostly given over to farming, which looks like the epitome of the tranquil English countryside. Yet there was a winter's day when it saw the greatest death toll of any single place in the United Kingdom, by a very long chalk. Blinded by snow, three muddled and largely non-uniformed armies hacked at one another until darkness fell, leaving so many dead that the Cock beck, which runs from Towton moor down to east Leeds, ran red with blood. Farmers and archaeologists still dig up bones cracked and scored with the vicious bludgeoning that constituted a medieval battle. An unusual sport of the wild rose grows in local hedges, known from its separate white and red colouring as the York and Lancaster. It is the best memorial of the Battle of Towton, fought at the height of the Wars of the Roses on Palm Sunday in 1461.

Nothing can match the estimated 30,000 English men and boys

who fell on those fields, but the country's landscape is formed in surprisingly large part by relics of similar violence, dating back to at least 4000BC, when stabbing and axe murders have been revealed by barrow-grave finds to have been part of prehistoric life on Salisbury plain. It is just as well to remember this, when tempted into rhapsodies by the beauty of our thatched cottages or the waving corn. As well as marking the hills with fortresses, and the maps with the crossed swords of battlefield sites, warfare has imposed a much wider pattern.

When I recently did the coast-to-coast walk from St Bees to Robin Hood's Bay, I was struck by the strange, deserted limestone plateau between Kirkby Stephen and Shap. Walkers are repeatedly advised to tread particularly carefully on this stretch and not to stray from the thread of a path that meanders across completely desolate grassland. It was not always empty. Through fear of invaders, this lofty refuge became the Manchester and Liverpool of our prehistoric ancestors. It is their fragile archaeological remains that hikers need to avoid. In the same way and for the same reasons, early civilisation laid out its first patterns in Yorkshire on the Pennine tops and the North York moors. For ramblers, grouse-shooters and the occasional sheep farmer who visit now, the sense of a violent, fortified past can be as potent as more obvious relics of quarrying and mining.

Later violent invasion by the Romans and Normans brought not just castles but also the feudal system, which created the underlying basis for the pattern of lowland farming today. At Laxton in Nottinghamshire, you can still see the original strip system in use and sense what life must have been for an Anglo-Saxon serf. Riots and bloodshed attended the next great change, the enclosure of communal land from the 17th century, which superimposed today's big fields on top of the feudal pattern. The motorway system is based on military roads designed to speed armies from the capital to rebellious regions, potential invasion coasts or the borders with

Scotland and Wales. The loss of manpower on the land to feed the terrible battles of 1914-18 began a revolution in farming that the need for efficient home production in 1939-45 completed. To subsume this history into a general knowledge of rural Britain is enriching and also a sound basis for considering what may, or should, happen next.

This is especially true because the story of the countryside is so often distorted by rose-embowered imagery. I have a valued book on my shelves called *The Truth about Cottages* by John Woodforde, which describes the reality behind the picturesque in an entertaining but scholarly way. As well as contributing to real history rather than embroidery, it is an invaluable manual for anyone involved in planning future rural housing, an abiding issue in the countryside. The stakes can be very high. I warmly recommend a typically energetic passage on this subject in Thomas De Quincey's *Recollections of the Lakes and Lake Poets*, where he contrasts the loveliness of Westmorland cottages built in a practical way, entirely influenced by purpose, position and local materials, with romantic follies that leak, look out of place and, in the case of Wordsworth's Allen Bank at Grasmere, have such impractically ornate chimneys that their irredeemable smokiness drove the famous tenant out.

One of the many subjects that fascinated me while compiling this collection was how germane to Britain this was in 1944, when the outcome of the second world war was no longer in doubt, and after grimly testing times the countryside was turning its attention to the future. There was much controversy about the Churchill government's plans for 'emergency cottages' to house the flood of ex-servicemen and women expected back in the countryside. They cost £1,000 each (£30,000 at today's values), which was widely considered profligate. They also seemed to have been designed by people who spent their lives in towns. In the zesty spirit of De Quincey, the

Women's Institutes of Northamptonshire organised a competition to come up with something better, which attracted 500 entries. The judges noted in a typical passage about practical experience v unrealistic dreaming: 'It is a false assumption that the average rural worker welcomes an almost all-glass south wall. He spends his whole day out of doors and when he returns home, he wants, first, somewhere to put his bicycle away, then a WC, somewhere to remove dirty boots and wet clothes and clean himself before entering the house proper. There he would like to find a fire doing an efficient job economically.'

Now this has very much the ring of a *Guardian* Country Diarist such as Major Arnold Boyd or Gwen McBryde, whose sound good sense you are about to get to know. Their concise paragraphs often notice architecture and social conditions. The wider landscape is of course their business too. And perhaps the greatest part of their interest is devoted to wildlife, plants as well as animals, and here the effects of war and violence also play an absorbing role. We do not have to go to the extreme example of the naturalist CP Castell, who for five years studied the gradual return of life to a second world war bomb crater on Bookham common in Surrey. You will find hundreds of more everyday references in this book to the way that a military event, or development, has attracted flora and fauna or driven them away. At Warcop ranges in Cumbria, the pounding of the hillsides by heavy artillery has created such friable earth that badgers have built setts far underground. Occasional collapses or direct hits are a price that evolution, through the survival of the fittest, can afford. Nightingales in London sang more loudly during the blitz. The blackout encouraged owls but deterred moths.

I hope that these writings will add to your enjoyment as you follow the diarists around, whether you are doing this in actuality and the fresh air (a most enjoyable hobby), or from the comfort of a fireside chair. My own travels have been greatly helped, as ever, by Amanda and Hexie Millais, my colleagues in the *Guardian* and *Observer*'s research department, Richard Nelsson, Amy Williams and Ruth Craven, the papers' Newsroom archive, the Leeds Library and both Leeds and Manchester reference libraries. If anyone can identify the diarists BA and MA I would be very pleased to hear from them. The very earliest part of my journey coincided with only the second-ever lunch held in London in honour of the *Guardian*'s Country Diarists, and they waxed eloquent. I am glad to have a good number of their contemporary contributions to give a sense of perspective, alongside the entries written when bombs were falling and the harvest was left to women and the elderly, prisoners of war and girls and boys.

Country remedies for war

ॐ June 1998 ॐ

Asked by the *Countryman* magazine in the spring of 1940 to say what 'pursuit, recreation, practice' they found most efficacious in yielding refreshment in those hard early days of the war, more than 40 well-known readers responded. Their replies reveal, on the whole, great common sense. Clement Attlee, for instance, resorted to 'vigorous forms of manual work' Bernard Shaw went about the lanes and woods with secateurs and sought to clear overgrown paths; the Hon Iris Mitford believed contact with the soil 'soothing and refreshing in any time of trouble' and Leslie Hore-Belisha, the secretary for war, relied on 'my farm'.

Such downright common sense is just as applicable today. Far too many townsfolk never get their hands dirty or bend their backs. After a day's double-digging, good old Sammy Dill slept like a log – 'mi back aches but not mi 'ead', he'd explain. I thought of Sammy Dill again the other day, crossing a grassy hillside near Langsett. Far below, towards the valley-bottom where the Little Don tumbles eastwards, we could make out a pair of old Vic Hallam poultry cotes – the sort that would each house about 40 birds and fitted with cast iron wheels allowing easy movement to avoid the sward being worn away around them – with the flock from each busy at work around the edges of the sunlit field. Happy the free range flock exploring their little empire, happy the owner crossing the field with a bucket of warm eggs. A dozen hens and a little field can keep a person happy all right. Sammy Dill again: 'Just watch yer birds busy before the sun goes down, that'll keep yer 'appy – and give yer a good neet's sleep!' The great portrait painter Eric Kennington sent in his suggestion to the *Countryman*, too, explaining his antidote for stress – 'building sheds for carts, trailers and bikes, repairing gates and sticking to the earth on all fours'. Wise man.

Roger Redfern

CHAPTER ONE

GHOSTS IN THE LANDSCAPE

In the course of five years as a teenage schoolboy, I was lucky to absorb all the main periods of history when warfare left its mark on the British countryside. Not in the classroom, although teachers kindled my enthusiasm, but out in the fields and woods themselves. Long ago, I used to wake up in the morning to the sight of the wedding-cake-shaped British Camp, also known as the Herefordshire Beacon, whose sensational earth ramparts brought the misty centuries of the Ancient Britons, Romans and Anglo-Saxons alive. Compared with Maiden Castle or Offa's Dyke, the Camp is surprisingly little-known and even in today's tourist-conscious Britain, it is scarcely promoted. That makes it all the more attractive for the explorer; you often have its windy summit to yourself, and the experience is vivid. The struggles that have shaped our landscape come alive in this turf-walled ring where desperate men with primitive weapons made last stands, from the fort's first building in the iron age, around 200BC, until Saxons and Britons reached a stand-off after the battle of Mount Badon in AD515.

A move then took me to Shrewsbury where I cycled out, full of anticipation, to the part of the town known as Battlefield. Like a South African family I later met in London, who had taken a bus marked 'St John's Wood' in the hope of finding some green open space, I was initially disappointed. The growth of modern Shrewsbury had embraced much of the open land where in 1403 King Henry IV trounced a rebel army led by the Percys of Northumberland in a battle typical of the conflict endemic in medieval 'Merrie' England. Owen Glendower was lurking in the wings to exploit any upset for the monarchy, which added to the significance of the rebels' defeat. Rushing traffic and modern offices initially suggested that there was little left besides the name. Completely wrongly. A lot of space was required for an estimated 50,000 men to engage in combat and a wander round the area on foot soon traced the likely battle lines, the graves and the sites where arrowheads and scraps of rusted armour were still being found.

It all did wonders for my appreciation of Shakespeare's *Henry IV Part 1*, whose cumbersome title has put off so many generations from its rewarding drama, which culminates in Harry Hotspur's death on Shrewsbury's battlefield. But then it was time to move again, northwards, for a summer of fishing for gudgeon and crayfish in the beck that winds from Golden Acre park to the centre of Leeds. The fish were forgotten when my brother and I unearthed a small, round slug of metal with a dent on one side from the muddy bank and discovered from a local historian that it was a civil war musket ball. For me, that third bloody period in the British countryside is brought to life, instantly, not by the famous battlefields of Naseby, Preston or Marston moor (which was also near home in Leeds) but in this quiet suburb where Sir William Saville's Royalists and 'Black Tom' Fairfax's Roundheads fought things out in a series of skirmishes between 1642 and 1644.

And so to the long, crumbling coast of Holderness in East Yorkshire, when a phone call to the *Guardian*'s Northern office alerted me to a second world war pillbox that was about to slide, in a particularly dramatic example of the constant cliff erosion, into the sea. Another local historian led me through the history of Britain's final period when warfare marked the countryside, albeit in the form of precautions rather than the spilling of blood. I learned the history of Napoleonic defences such as the Martello towers, 103 of them built between 1804 and 1812 along the shore from Aldeborough to Seaford. Why 'Martello', which is the Italian for hammer? It was a corruption of Mortella (or Myrtle) Point in Corsica, where the squat, circular design of a French fort so impressed the British government that they used it for their own defences.

Thus knowledge is passed on. And my East Riding mentor was equally full of data on the pillbox system, knew all about the military wrecks on this part of the coast (including the skeleton of a German submarine) and could explain which chunks of concrete and iron on the beach were part of the line of traps that awaited any seaborne Nazi invasion. I later discovered for myself the concrete 'ears', which listened out for potential invaders on the south coast and the more recent cold war systems on Orford Ness in Suffolk, one of the most fascinating of modern 'warfare sites' which – for now, at least – complete a pattern that began with prehistoric earthworks on the moors inland.

This personal odyssey is one that any of us can take, learning in the process how centuries of conflict have shaped the countryside. There are different clues for each of them: the constant warfare of prehistoric, Roman and dark age times; the scarcely less settled

medieval period, when apart from civil strife there were two successful seaborne invasions, by the future kings Henry IV and Henry VII
in 1399 and 1485; the civil war; and preparations for invasion or
bombardment by air, missiles or terrorists between Napoleon and
the present day. As a subtext, the countryside has also seen lesser
unrest from demonstrations, rick-burnings and riots throughout its
history. To start unravelling the story, spend an hour or so with your
local 1:25,000 Ordnance Survey map and see how many military
references you find. Castle, fort, moat and camp are obvious, and
sometimes helpfully printed in Gothic type as antiquities; but soon
you learn how to trace the more hidden clues. Any placename
ending in 'borough' or 'brough' comes from the Old English *burh*
meaning fort. Chesters and -casters (and of course castles) derive in
the same way from the Latin *castra*, meaning a camp, and show
where Roman legionaries were stationed. Wapentake, the old division of a shire, is entirely military: the 'weapon collection' for raising
troops. The common term 'butt' or 'butts' in or near villages marks
a site used for archery practice in the heyday of the English longbow.

This was compulsory on Sundays for many years in medieval and
Tudor times, even if attendance was not always keen. In 1549,
during one of many French invasion scares, Bishop Latimer
preached a sermon on the longbow as 'God's instrument whereby
he hath given us many victories against our enemies.' His main
purpose was to reinvigorate justices of the peace who had ' ...been
negligent in executing the law so that everyone has gone whoring
into the towns instead of shooting in the fields'.

Taking the map out with you for a walk, you can continue explo-
rations on foot. Those yew trees by the village church may be descen-
dants of the Agincourt bowmen's original local arsenals: yew is
particularly good for making hard but springy bows. The trees were
often grown in churchyards because their berries could be poisonous

to the livestock that the walls around the graves kept out. Look for clues on the headstones, too, and in the memorials and effigies inside the church. I was recently at Rousham, the beautiful mansion in grounds by William Kent near Oxford, which has a poignant example: standard Commonwealth War Graves Commission headstones for two sons of the Cottrell Dormer family, which has lived here since 1635 and still does. The lads died in the trenches in 1914 and 1915, still in their early 20s, instead of returning to manage the paradise where they had been brought up; a small but telling part of the momentous changes brought by the first world war.

Part of the fascination of detective work is discovering how prominent many of the now obscure traces of conflict once were, just as more obvious reminders of warfare were even more striking in past times. A Norman castle retains an air of command today, but nothing like the brutality it would have had when newly built. Historians believe that many of them, like the Roman wall, were lime-washed to make their role as bastions of authority and occupation visible from miles away. The 14th-century Welsh bard Daffyd ap Gwyllim is a witness, via a poem in which he compares his girlfriend to a sunbeam striking the walls of a whitewashed English fort. They were the equivalent of the British army's fortified bases in Northern Ireland, which at the time of writing are being recorded for their own place in the history of arms and the countryside.

A message beacon, by contrast, is something a rambler in the countryside might miss; yet the chain of hilltop fires formed a highly sophisticated military call-up system that also left its mark on the land. Not only in the actual beacons but also in the maintenance of clear lines of sight between them, so that different signals could raise trained bands along the south coast or bring reinforcements from Gloucestershire and other counties further inland. It worked. As late as 1804, a false alarm during a period of regular Napoleonic invasion scares led to the firing of the beacon at Hume Castle in Berwickshire. The chain was set off and the county volunteers turned out everywhere.

The structure of a battlefield is also vulnerable to time's effects, but you can still see the sloping open land essential for successful cavalry charges, as at Marston moor in 1644 or Lansdown the year earlier, or the copses and spinneys used by armies for cover. History records other clues; the battlefield at Stratton in North Cornwall was reckoned locally to be so fertilised by blood and guts that it produced an exceptional 60 bushels of barley to the acre for many years after the fighting was over in 1643. There is the different harvest, too, of archaeological finds and military remains, even if local villagers have had a reputation throughout Britain's history for stripping a battlefield of everything with any value. The only battlefield that may never give anything up, if it is ever located somewhere near Mold in North Wales, is the site of the alleged 'Hallelujah Victory' of AD430, when a Romano-British army hid in ambush and then jumped up and shouted 'Hallelujah!' three times so loudly that the Saxons ran away and no one was killed on either side.

The *Guardian's* Country Diarists have an eye for such things, and like the references to conflict in place names on maps or the lie of once-entrenched or fortified land, the scale of their interest becomes clear when you start looking for it. Here is a sample as a prelude, before we move on to entries actually written during the two great conflicts of the 20th century.

Fort, castle and munition mine

∾ SEPTEMBER 2005 ∾

Bright-pink bell heather and paler ling, spikes of bleached grass and prickly thickets hide the pits, dumps and shafts of old mines and quarries on top of Kit hill in the Tamar valley. A path along a part-filled costeaning trench crosses a shady, fern-growing adit from the last working mine, where tin and wolfram were dug out during the first world war. This granite hill, set between Dartmoor and Bodmin moor, is now managed as a country park but it has always been a focus and distinctive landmark. The present-day summit stack was the chimney for an adjoining beam engine house, built in 1858 and originally whitewashed to act as a day mark visible from the sea. For a short time previous a windmill drained this mine, but it was blown away in a storm. In the 18th century Sir John Call had built a folly, a mock Danish castle on the hilltop, visible from his mansion at Whiteford and pictured on a pound note. In earlier times, surrounding dwellers would have looked up towards the site of beacons lit to raise alarm, muster the militia and celebrate midsummer. A fort was constructed during the civil war and, even earlier, the large bronze age barrow would have been prominent.

A toll road, built in 1928, brought trippers to the summit – to a car park, putting green and cafe. Today there is no parking within the historic sites but people can stroll and gaze towards the distance as their dogs and children run and scramble over the grassy banks. A savoury smell drifts uphill from Callington's pasty factory. The sun draws up water as it sinks towards Stowe's hill and patches of light, shade and rising mist enliven the post-harvest panorama.

Virginia Spiers

The brave pipers

ℬ MARCH 2004 ℭ

Pipe bands are still an important part of the heritage of market towns in northern Britain. The office of piper was, and still is, often hereditary, the skills either with pipe or drum passed down from father to son. A 16th-century account compares the bagpipe with the harp: the one for war, the other for peace. Many amateur bands, especially in Yorkshire and Lancashire, consisted mostly of working men engaged in mills, iron works or collieries, and the demand from the army for martial music helped keep bands going.

The rules of the music are still not all known; they are presumed to relate to those of Gaelic poetry because when the official order of poets fell into decay it was then that piping families began to grow in importance. The British army went into the first world war with seven pipe bands and came out of it with more than 100, so potent was their skirl and drone at driving men over the top. In the second world war, one piper won the Victoria Cross for continuing to play while lying on the sand mortally wounded at El Alamein. Today, the British army has two pipe bands, Highland and Lowland, but martial music is still used to keep regiments in step and morale high.

There has been a pipe band in our market town of Morpeth since 1913, and it still plays today. 'The Morpeth Pipe Band has played for all civic occasions in the borough here since the mid-1930s and we have never missed one,' Stewart Todd, the secretary, told me. A friend told me that the way to enjoy pipe bands is from a safe distance. Well, she is not a Geordie, and next time our pipe band are on parade I shall give them an extra cheer. They are part of our heritage.

Veronica Heath

Hiding the soldiers

ೞ JUNE 1999 ೞ

St Buryan's high granite tower, on its churchyard mound, is the focus for Penwith's ancient landscape towards Land's End. Narrow roads radiate through silken barley, sturdy potatoes, grass and buttercups, old paths crossing massive hedgebanks and little streams. Green lanes are linear woods, trodden ways engulfed in cow parsley, gorse, bramble, overarching sloe and willow.

Off one of those tracks, in a clearing of brilliant, late bluebells, is Boscawen Un, a megalithic circle around a leaning central stone. About this open site, scarlet sorrel, sweet vernal grass, pink campion and foxglove grow through bracken beneath Creeg Tol. A cuckoo calls persistently from thick, white hawthorns and droning forage harvesters pick up wilted grass from neighbouring fields, making silage for one of the few remaining, traditional Guernsey herds.

Just north is Carn Euny, the remains of an iron age village, set on a south-westerly slope below Caer Bran fort, overlooking the expansive windswept plateau of small fields and narrow wooded valleys above the off-lying, hazy sea. Excavated in the 1920s and 60s, mounds, pavements and low walls, sprouting spiky flowers of pennywort, delineate the earliest round houses and later courtyard dwellings. Within the dark fogou, an underground passage of drystone walls and huge granite lintels, sun shines through a modern roof grid, lighting up patches of phosphorescent moss in the circular side chamber.

Nearby, through a thicket of pink and white Penzance briars, steep steps lead down to Chapel well, clear water gushing below ferns and mossy stones, adjoining the site of St Eunius chapel. Holy wells have reputations for healing and there are tales of witches in the mysterious subterranean spaces. A long-distant ancestor, Arthus

Levelis of Trewoofe, met a coven in a fogou in Lamorna valley. He also hid 12 Royalist soldiers there in the civil war. He died in 1671, 'the last of his name'. His daughter Prudence married Richard Vosper of Liskeard, 80 miles nearer the Tamar valley.

Virginia Spiers

Blind man's fort

ॐ APRIL 1999 ॐ

We were scanning the lower slopes of Brent Knoll (the great mound that rears unexpectedly up to a height of 135m, dominating the surrounding coastal flats near Burnham) and looking for the best way to the top. A man with a white stick approached at a brisk pace. He made his way directly on a diagonal connecting the stiles at opposite corners of a field and skipped nimbly over the one beside us. I asked him the name of the church with the thin spire behind him. 'That's East Knoll,' he said, turning and pointing directly at it. Then he spun round and pointed the opposite way: 'That's West Knoll, where I went to school. I'm registered blind, but I've lived here all my life.' On the slopes, the pasture was beginning to look green and lush, with plenty of celandine, and daisies everywhere, signs of spring, though as yet there were no cattle out to graze. The untidy fringe of scrub that encircles the top of the hill was festooned with sprays of white where the blackthorn was in flower. Above the scrub and up a short, steeper climb, we came to impressive earthworks. A double ditch and ramparts reinforced with stone surround an iron age fort that covers one and a half hectares. This place was an ancient refuge for man and beast from enemies or flood (during the civil war, unruly Royalist soldiers pillaged the low-lying settlements) and it is a commanding site where you hope for glittering views across the sea to the Welsh hills, and inland over miles of flatland to the Mendips and beyond Glastonbury Tor. But it was a dank morning when we were there. The seaward view was dull and mysterious. Stert flats to our left and Berrow flats to our right barely showed as thin strips of a slightly darker grey than that of the still water. Inland, when the mist shifted, there was an occasional blue hint of the outline of distant hills. On the top we found few signs of the buildings said to have stood there. Only a tall mast stands at one side of the fort, and at the other, a stout, stone monument celebrating Queen Victoria's Jubilee and three subsequent coronations.

John Vallins

Guns, bombs and a sword

ℰ FEBRUARY 2001 ℭ

A King Canute coin of 1035 was found last year in Limerick City South during excavations near the rivers Shannon and Abbey. I find archaeological discoveries deeply satisfying, a marriage between the factual and the imaginative. In these same excavations, still in progress, were also found a well-preserved *fulacht fiadh* (cooking place), a Viking zoomorphic mound, a spur and silver groat minted in Calais (Henry VI), a port seal of the 16th century, mortar bombs, and a beautifully decorated sword hilt of the Williamite wars, as well as revolvers and a hand grenade from our own civil war. What a historical sequence, all in the same tight-knit location, portraying human occupations, cooking, trading, making war, and its corollary, killing. What busy creatures lived and died there? What hopes and fears filled their hearts? And now, whether full of importance or lowly in their living, their 'little lives are rounded with a sleep'.

Such were my musings as I stood beside our nearest *fulacht fiadh*, a green mound with a round cut in one side, near the O'Loughlin castle of Gleninagh, each separated in time, both so close to the ocean's edge. As I walked by the sea I saw its excavatory efforts: stones and shells flung by raging tides, a bright yellow bucket, one canvas shoe. I turn for home and after the last round of the road I see spread before me, as if for the first time, a few of Ballyvaughan's rooftops and the small green fields ascending in their infinity of shapes, bordered by the simple dry-stone walls, limited by the stark beauty of the limestone hills whose line I follow to the Flaggy Shore and its Martello tower.

Sarah Poyntz

Phantom spears

ᏸ᎓ MARCH 2000 ᏣᏛ

High above the village of Clee St Margaret, where the Clee brook runs down the main street, the skylarks rise through warm hazy sunlight. The track from Stokegorse across the Yeld follows old ways sunk under bracken and centuries of history. Breeze from the west swings over this shoulder of the Brown Clee hill, over the wild expanse of grass and bracken commons called Clee Liberty and Abdon Liberty, which are the steep hillsides of the twin peaks of Brown Clee and Abdon Burf. On the lower slopes the boundary hedges are of ancient and solid holly, once used for winter cattle food.

The commons are packed now with sheep, so many that the sward is battered to bowling-green height and nothing, except bracken, grows more than an inch high. Great swaths of dry bracken have been mowed and together with the relentless grinding teeth of sheep, the strange topography of the land is exposed. There are remains of sunken lanes with banks on either side, quarry-holes with slabs of a old red sandstone poking out, odd formations of ditches, mounds and plateaux.

This land has been shaped by centuries of human labour; time and vegetation have a levelling effect and you can't tell immediately whether these ground forms are decades or centuries in age. But when you see the hill fort of Nordy Bank you know you are in a landscape that has been occupied since the iron age. The fort is on a flat promontory jutting westwards from the hill. Its earthwork ring and ditch are impressive even after two and a half thousand years. Once faced with sandstone from surrounding pits, which still show through the soil of the wall, it would have been topped with a formidable palisade. The scattered farms and smallholdings are probably what remain of ancient settlements that looked to this place as sanctuary in times of trouble and the locus of their culture in this landscape.

As the skylarks rise from the noises of a working countryside, above Nordy Bank, the sky is shattered by the war-like blattering of a huge military helicopter. It swoops low, hawking, as if searching for insurgence in the wild Liberties. The ghosts of Nordy Bank reach for their spears.

Paul Evans

King Arthur and Dad's Army

❧ JUNE 2002 ❧

The Preseli hills mark Pembrokeshire. Foel Cwmcerwyn, at 536m the highest point in west Wales, is one of many tops that form the hills. You wander over dry moorland and wet bog land at any time of year. With no compass, you can walk in circles for hours if the cloud comes down. This sounds awful, but they have a seductive appeal quite unrelated to size and terrain.

It is here that you find one of Arthur's graves, and on Cerrigmarchogion – the rocks of the knights – the resting place of his knights killed by Twrch, the black boar, and turned into stone. And there's a river of stone, which the local wildlife trust was exploring.

For geological reasons – various hypotheses – there is a clearly marked trail of huge boulders, with water below running down the side of the hill. At its source, there's a cromlech capstone. Was it dropped by a glacier or tossed by Arthur? Was it used? Questions in this magical area are happily more common than answers. The larks and meadow pipits singing around us sufficed.

With a cold wind and unwilling sun, the butterwort waited for warmth, but the round-leaved sundew and tiny cranberry were in flower. Stands of firclub moss radiated cheerfulness, while the beech-fern glowed with its modest, downturned base pinnae. Deep in the gaps between the boulders were delicate examples of Wilson's filmy fern, looking less moss-like than usual.

We ate lunch at Carn Bica, where what is probably a bronze age burial mound has been rearranged over time, most recently by the Home Guard in the second world war – or Arthur rising to fight? Cold and bleak, but sitting on a huge stone, was a grey squirrel. A fully grown drinker moth caterpillar was there to find a safe spot to pupate. Another outing took us to count bee orchids on Newport sand-dunes. We found approximately 682. Each year, we do this. A hypothesis will appear soon. Meantime, the clear fact is that the volunteers enjoy the counting.

Audrey Insch

Traces of conflict

ॐ JULY 2005 ॐ

From the sun-dappled and translucent river Lynher, dusty paths lead uphill through ferns, oaks and hollies. Above steep thistly enclosures, with hedges draped in lady's bedstraw and festooned with honeysuckle, and beyond Bowdanoddan's conifers, the granite moor is verdant. Sharp edges of worked moor stone and boulders like beached whales are part submerged in cushions of ling and whortleberry, interspersed with the blue-green new growth of gorse and springy turf starred with tormentil. A kestrel hovers by Hawk's tor, below the summit of domed and dished rocks (called devil's punchbowls in Cornwall and virgins' bidets in Brittany). From this lookout, the listening 'saucers' of far-off Morwenstow's tracking station float above a heat haze. Dartmoor is pale and blue, the intervening pastures, scattered cornfields and stubble crisscrossed with tree-topped banks.

Downhill, beyond a thicket of invasive rhododendron, a herd of hefted cattle lie content beside Withey brook and, from the other side of the tor, carries the sound of voices, of visitors walking to Trewortha's reconstructed and thatched roundhouses close to ancient hut circles. The village of North Hill appears tucked away in greenery. Nearby Trebartha Hall was demolished after serving as a hospital during the second world war. Slate and painted monuments in the church commemorate the family of Spoures and Rodds, who were connected with this estate from the Conquest until 1940.

We pass down into the valley, under shady beeches within earshot of the waterfall, and look back to the eastern escarpment of Bodmin moor, where flowering chestnuts gleam pale gold in the afternoon sun.

Virginia Spiers

Target practice

ᘒ JULY 2005 ᘓ

A friend's house is built of stone brought from the ruins of Thornseat Delf, a former lonely moorside farm hidden from the general gaze high on the Bradfield moors, west of Sheffield. Long abandoned as a dwelling, Thornseat Delf was used for artillery practice in the last war and stood as a ruin until the stone was carted away in the past two decades.

Thornseat Road is the name of the track that climbs to the 420m heathery knob behind the ruin site. It's edged with foxglove spires and overhung with creamy plates of elder blooms; below the moor's edge the last conifers fell behind and we stride the open ground, the very personification of freedom. A slanting line of shooting butts decked with the fresh greenery of bilberry foliage guided us up to the crest of Wet Slack ridge. Our goal was New Cross, crowning this gentle ridge-top and not easy to locate since its stone shaft was vandalised in the 90s. Only the base marks the spot, close to a pretty pool that on this day had quite dried out.

The heat made the hazy views vague. The hares we saw made unusually relaxed getaways across the heather crests. A westward traverse brought us to the barren Middle Moss. At least its brittle-dry heather coat made for easy going under the burning sunshine. We came to the watershed and a tremendous vista to the west, down Cranberry Clough and Upper Hey to Derwent Dale and the vague, grey lift of eastern Bleaklow.

A short pull to the south and we stood at the tiny cairn upon High Stones. At 550m this is the highest point in South Yorkshire, 4m loftier than its northern neighbour, Margery Hill, which is often claimed as the high point.

Roger Redfern

Wartime sweethearts

ℰℴ JANUARY 2005 ℂℛ

We lost two old acquaintances in Bishop Auckland during the January gales. Not people, I hasten to add, but beech trees. Two of a row of five whose roots seemed to melt into a steep bank under soaring canopies that shaded the path. Trees that we looked forward to seeing whenever we passed by. Reliable, familiar landmarks. Weakened by bracket fungi, one snapped at head height, crashing down in a jumble of splintered branches. The other simply tipped over on its rotten roots and slid down the bank, inflicting a mortal blow on a third as it fell.

We'll miss them as much for the inscriptions they carried, with hints of untold stories, as for their physical presence. Since at least 1935, the oldest dated initials, generations of local couples have proclaimed their mutual affection here by carving hearts and arrows in the smooth grey bark. 'Billy loves Jane for ever' dates from June 3 1966, when we were 15-year-olds, the Kinks' Sunny Afternoon and the Beatles' Paperback Writer were riding high in the charts and England's World Cup win was just six weeks away. Did Billy propose to Jane under this tree that summer day, then inscribe the date to commemorate her consent? Whatever became of them? And did earlier lovers who carved their names here during the second world war survive the conflict and live to show grandchildren the place where they plighted their troth?

There are those who deplore the practice of carving names in trees. I suppose that the accumulated wounds on these beeches may well have let in fungal spores that led to their eventual downfall. But without the names they would just be two more anonymous victims of a gale.

Phil Gates

Out of bounds

ℰᴼ MARCH 2000 ℚℛ

Tottington doesn't really exist at all now. Nor can you even go to look at its bomb-damaged ruins, because they lie within the MoD's Stanford training area, an 8,900-hectare block of south Norfolk where access is strictly prohibited. Yet until the second world war, Tottington had a thriving population of more than 200, and the history of the place has been described in an excellent new book, *Tottington: A Lost Norfolk Village*, by Hilda and Edmund Perry (George Reeve, £12.95). A former resident, 88-year-old Hilda Perry has recalled the pre-war period in minute detail, along with its long-vanished way of life.

It was a world in which her father had a full-time job looking after the adjacent farm's principal agricultural equipment (the team of heavy horses) and in which a labourer's wages were 25 shillings for a 50-hour week. By contrast, the local landowner thought himself too broke to live in his own Merton Hall and stayed in a nearby house while spending £10,000 a year on the estate's pheasant shoot.

Generously illustrated throughout and including meticulously researched genealogies, the bulk of the book provides an intimate portrait of a close-knit rural community. And this acts as an emotional context in which to comprehend the Perry family's sudden eviction, along with 800 other residents from five villages, in 1942.

The country needed space for training soldiers and this part of Breckland was earmarked for requisition by the War Department. The tenants were expected to uproot their lives in just 10 days but this was eventually extended to four weeks. Although there were promises of a return once the conflict ended, the residents never went back. The postwar Labour government decided the nation still needed training areas to meet the new threat from the eastern bloc. Ironically, the authoritarian methods of communism raised their own kind of monument on Tottington's grave, when the MoD built a replica East German village, at a cost of £4m, to train our troops in the arts of urban warfare.

Mark Cocker

A military sanctuary

In these last days of May, the lanes around my Cheshire village are a mass of white blossom: the hawthorns are in full bloom and the verges are dominated by the first of the roadside umbellifers – the feathery-leaved cow parsley, whose frothy appearance probably gave rise to its folk-name, Queen Anne's lace. Competing for space between the tall parsley plants is the hedge garlic with its light-green, heart-shaped leaves and pungent smell, but the brightest of all are the star-shaped petals of the greater stitchwort. This straggly plant, with angled stems, clambers through the vegetation, relying on neighbouring grasses and flowers for support. Each stretch of roadside is patrolled by the spring butterflies: orange tip, which is the most numerous, small tortoiseshell, peacock, and – in the past few days – the cinnabar moths have appeared there, bright-red markings serving as a warning to would-be predators that they are poisonous. Hence their slow, leisurely flight along the hedgerows searching for ragwort or groundsell on which to lay this year's batch of eggs.

Some four miles out of the village lies the site of a former second world war MoD unit that, with all its buildings long since demolished, has developed into an area of scrubby, rough grassland, the kind of habitat that has almost vanished under a multitude of out-of-town shopping centres. It was here, two days ago, that a colleague and I stood for a good hour and counted six skylarks rising high into the sky, each in turn singing and eventually falling back towards their territories like tiny parachutes with legs dangling beneath them. We also found reed bunting, linnet, and breeding lapwing, all species under threat because of the disappearance of their specialist habitat.

Would this site still be here next year, we asked ourselves?

John Thompson

Tank tracks

ᔕᓇ AUGUST 1997 ᣍᔕ

Swallows curled in the stiff, west breeze above the top of the green hill, omens of high summer in the great skies over these Pennine moorlands. We came along the lane to Upper Midhope, where the broad concrete road is still a reminder of the tank training ground prepared here above the Little Porter valley, just too late to be of any use at the end of the last war. No tanks ever rumbled here at the edge of the moors, no dust blew up in their tracks to cloak the mellow walls of Hawksworth House. When the late Helen Edith Green moved here from the Waggon and Horses Inn in 1960 she filled the place with antiques: eminently suitable for a house that was part cruck-timbered, part Georgian. One of the interior windows contains Bolsterstone glass, so fragile that it bends when pressed. Now that she and her bachelor sons have died, this upper end of moorside Upper Midhope is not the same: there's little continuity with the hard, romantic times of the 20s and 30s. There is some continuity, however, if we take the narrow, sunken lane below the lower part of the village. Though the poultry flock has gone from their wheeled cote on the tilting bank near the keeper's labrador pens, we can still discover the juicy colony of pink purslane (*Claytonia alsinoides*) that decks the laneside between April and July.

This smooth and fleshy annual must have haunted this shady corner for centuries, overlooking the paved way where the Midhope cattle have come to drink at the stone trough, fern-edged, morning and night for countless summers. We looked out from this green nook towards the south, to the hollows and knolls of Midhope moors and espied the first mauve blush upon their cheeks. The heather blooms were working their magic again, turning the old Derwent cart road (Cut Gate) into a Royal Mile.

Roger Redfern

The lost air-raid shelters

ꙮ JUNE 1998 ꙮ

Farmers here in Northumberland are busy with sheep-shearing. Small, one-man contractors using portable electric clippers set up on trailers and make a seasonal living with several thousand sheep sheared every week. The shearing can vary from year to year – when the weather has been kind and there is a good rise in the wool, the shears run smoothly. A strong, protesting sheep is an awkward creature to handle but an experienced shearer is a marvel to watch and handles each struggling beast with such skill that there is minimum trauma – it is stripped within minutes. While the ewes are sheared, the lambs in an adjacent pen are wormed and a hand, usually a woman, is in charge of wrapping the wool into neat bundles. Two lambs from a neighbour are earmarked for my freezer when the grandchildren come in August, though I prefer not to know which ones they are. He will bring them butchered just as I want them, and my elderflower champagne will be ready by then, so we will enjoy a glass from the fridge and a gossip. The elderflowers are very good this month, aided by heavy rains and now warmth and hot sun. I have just made 16 pints, which will be ready in eight weeks. Our land is old meadow, which has never seen the plough, and there has been a wealth of wildflowers this year. Down the west side of the big field are depressions now grassed over – the air-raid shelters dug by the villagers in the last war. A metal detector asked permission to probe in the field and unearthed an interesting collection of buttons, coins and bottle tops, so they must have been used at some time, although fortunately not as a place of refuge. More likely children in the parish were exploring until their elders put a stop to it.

Veronica Heath

Churchill at Gumstool Hill

❧ NOVEMBER 1998 ❧

Jackdaws noisily disputing their territorial rights to a visibly crumbling brick chimney that stands above a roof of traditional Cotswold stone tiles are a regular morning spectacle as the November sun lights up the Tetbury roofscape. The black, spectral figures rise into the air from the roof ridge to the west of us, flapping angrily and squawking as they try to reclaim what can only be a nesting site – and which they do not actually need for some months.

Against a blue, winter sky, with mellow limestone below, it is almost a medieval scene, enacted every morning high above our courtyard garden. This garden is itself of some historic interest, for we back on to the Malthouse, a building that is now in community use, but which during the second world war was used by the US Sixth Army. In May 1945, the large open space of the floor of the Malthouse was used by military technicians to construct a 3D panorama model of the stretch of French coastline that became known as Omaha beach, and Churchill and Eisenhower came to

Hundreds of concrete pillboxes remain from world war two defences

Tetbury to view the representation of what, a month later, would become one of the most vigorously resisted of the invasion beaches.

The war leaders arrived in Tetbury by train, something that is no longer possible, and walked up Gumstool Hill from the now defunct station after their steam train journey on the branch line from Kemble. With luck, this branch line may see a new lease of life as a cycle track to Cirencester in the not too distant future. They approached the Malthouse through its back door, which is in our garden, and this historic bit of Cotswold stone, which now hosts brownies and play groups, played a part in the successful military planning of the invasion.

We can look out of the kitchen door to the cobbles over which these famous feet trod at a momentous time in our destiny.

Colin Luckhurst

Scramble, scramble

ஐ OCTOBER 2003 ௸

The A30 runs eastwards out of Somerset towards Shaftesbury's hill town, across what was once marshland and along what older maps call the Sherborne Causeway. I could see a couple of horses in one low-lying field there, a few cows in another, and three buses decaying in a patch of weeds. Big corrugated hangars and small red-brick buildings showed where, during the war, the flat farmland was requisitioned to make an airfield. Round the corner of a hangar, I came upon a smart, yellow helicopter marked 'Dorset and Somerset Air Ambulance'. The crew (two paramedics and the pilot) wait there, like fighter crews in films, for the 'Scramble' klaxon, and they reckon to be airborne in three minutes, on the way to a cardiac arrest on a remote golf course, a difficult birth in an inaccessible farmhouse, a horse rider's broken leg, a farm worker's limb crushed by an overturned tractor, or an injured walker on a trackless Quantock moor or precipitous Dorset coastal path. And of course there are the traffic accidents, where the little aircraft can thread swiftly in and out. Two patients can be stowed from the tail end, and swivel chairs enable the paramedics to apply their skills and a remarkable range of tightly packed equipment to the patients' needs on the way to 'definitive care' in hospital. The crew must make quick decisions. Should they fly to Dorchester's new hospital with its helipad or Salisbury with its specialist burns and spinal units? Tied to a lamp-post at Henstridge crossroads, a handwritten notice invited passersby to a dance in the village hall to raise funds to help sustain the work of our air-ambulance.

John Vallins

CHAPTER TWO

SILENT FIELDS

The *Guardian* Country Diary began in March 1904, a time
when Britain was at the height of her powers but suffering
regular bouts of nerves about whether her empire was one on which
the sun might one day really set. The United States was a bumptious
and clearly potent challenger, but still very distant at a time when the
fastest crossing of the Atlantic took more than five days. The great
European powers were another matter; close and jealous. Although
the Royal Navy patrolled the distant seas magnificently, there was a
recurring nightmare in the national psyche about a surprise invasion
on the mother country herself, a leap across what were known
with good reason as the Narrow Seas. It was a nightmare in which
the violation of the English countryside played a central part.
Among a spate of invasion novels was one called *The Battle of
Dorking*, a title that summed up these fears. It was accompanied by

much pulp literature but also some lasting books that testify to the depth of invasion scare worries, notably John Buchan's *The Thirty-Nine Steps* and Erskine Childers' *The Riddle of the Sands*.

Central to the plots was the sweet softness of the main victim, the English countryside, the home of yeomen with sturdy values, and traditions that continued to flourish, from fox-hunting to labour hiring fairs. The sense of menace was heightened by an actual devastation that had only recently taken place, often overlooked today but described in detail then by the *Manchester Guardian*. The 50-odd years between the arrival of the railways and the production of the country's first motor cars saw an extraordinary slump in the economy of villages and small towns. The cart and carriage trade simply disappeared. It was a transport hiccup, in retrospect, because renewed prosperity returned on a much larger scale with the car. But at the time, the shift of goods and people to the railways was ruinous. Instructively, the *Manchester Guardian* compared its effects to exactly the sort of invasion that the *Battle of Dorking*'s author Lt Col Sir George Tomkyns described.

In a series entitled *Rambles Around Manchester* (newspaper headlines were modest and calm in those days), the paper wrote of '…fields and meadows looking as unkempt and disused as if they had been ravaged by an invading army'. The picture of gloom touched on a deeper malaise in the conservative world of British farming. After a radical surge in the late 18th century, when a series of poor harvests and resulting bread riots led to innovations in agriculture, the countryside had settled into comfortable routine. Enclosures, 'Turnip' Townsend and Arthur Young, the sedulous researcher into better ways of farming, were distant memories. Initiative had passed to the towns with their successive industrial revolutions. Wage differentials attracted anyone with gumption to try their luck in the city rather than slog in the fields for life. Imperial trade took up the slack in food production for the country's growing population. The cities were teeming but there was plenty of wheat in Canada.

That was the world of mass production. By contrast, craftsmanship and the maintenance of tradition were what mattered to rural society. Tools were ancient but beautifully maintained and there was a rhythm to life and respect for nature that have nostalgic echoes in the modern Green movement. When *Country Life* magazine commissioned a writer to bicycle from Perranporth in Cornwall to Cromer in Norfolk for a series on rural change, what struck him most was the way farmers clung to the horse. If they did have a machine and it went wrong, he wrote, ' ... their instinct is to leave it to rust beside the hedge.' Life was careful and slow. Hayricks were often given time-consuming caps twined from straw into individual patterns. In the 1960s, a retired farmworker in his 80s told RE Moreau, author of *The Departed Village*: 'People didn't know no different than to just keep jiggeting along; and whatever they were doing, they were interested in. People were more civilised then.' One statistic among the millions compiled for rural output tells the story: the harvesting of timber in the 19th century and up to 1914 was so lethargic, in spite of demand for pit props, ships' decking and other uses, that even the huge felling programmes of the first and second world wars, combined, did not make up for the shortfall. There just seemed to be all the time in the world.

In fact, time was running out. The international jitters that built the arsenals of Germany, Russia, Austro-Hungary and France, and led Britain to have a policy of maintaining a battleship fleet as big as those of the next two navies combined, came close to triggering war in a series of diplomatic incidents between 1900 and the eventual cataclysm in 1914. The continental powers were constantly debating whether the best 'defensive' strategy was to strike first, even though their leaders understood the risk of general ruin. The

German chancellor, Theodor von Bethmann-Hollweg, confided longingly in a colleague in 1913: 'I am fed up with war and the clamour for war and the perpetual armaments. It is high time that the great nations calmed down again and occupied themselves with peaceful pursuits, or there will be an explosion which no one desires and which will be to the detriment of all.' With similar foresight, the rural novelist and poet Thomas Hardy mourned the consequences of waging war between 'kin folk, kin-tongued as we are' in his poem *The Pity of It* whose title foreshadowed Wilfred Owen's famous lines: 'My subject is war and the pity of war. The poetry is in the pity.'

The situation was made more dangerous by alliances and commitments that were part of the attempt by the rival empires to deter one another from aggression, but appeared in their mirror image as plots to isolate. In the end, they dragged Europe into the abyss. A Balkan nationalist assassinated the heir to the Austro-Hungarian empire, which declared war on Serbia, invoking an alliance with Germany, while Russia honoured agreements with Serbia, which brought in France and then its ally the British Empire.

Everywhere, troops mobilised and trains moved; and in the villages of Britain the young men queued to join up. Before the end of August, many of them who had previously seen the next shire as foreign territory were in a different country for the first time. Newspaper reporters described their arrival in Boulogne: 'Every man in the prime of life, shirts open at the front and as they shout and sing you can see the working of the muscles of their throats, their wide open mouths and rows of dazzling teeth. Every movement spells fitness for the field … '

But not for the fields that needed them at home. The harvest was only partly in; the designs for the year's new hayrick tops were incomplete. It was a situation paralleled in the newspaper world, where the daily routines were suddenly turned upside down by the arrival of war. Like a little hamlet itself, the *Manchester Guardian*'s Country Diary was not immune. It had celebrated its 10th anniversary in February 1914, pottering along for most of the decade in the single, capable hands of Thomas Coward, a retired textile bleacher from Cheshire who taught himself to become Britain's leading authority on birds. He passed on his observations, mostly of Cheshire wildlife, in concise paragraphs that stimulated dozens of other enthusiasts to write in and have their own findings described. Coward's column was frequently interrupted by messages to this network – 'AFC – it will have been a buzzard', 'PBS of Stalybridge: I suggest a sooty tern' – while behind the scenes he had been conducting a heartfelt correspondence with the newspaper's famous editor CP Scott.

This related to Scott's growing feeling that the diary should have a variety of authors, a threat to Coward's weekly earnings of 30 shillings (£105 today) for six columns of some 250 words each. Schooled in patience by long hours in the bird hides that still overlook his favourite Cheshire meres, Coward conducted diplomacy on the lines of the European powers. He used his wife's ill health, made pointed allusions to his other freelance employers such as the *Scotsman*, and worried that erroneous views about country matters, especially the great debate over whether pigeons and rooks were pests or friends of the farmer, might undermine the diary. But in the end, he had to accede and share the week with another retired Manchester businessman, Arthur Nicholson, who took over the column on Tuesdays, Thursdays and Saturdays from October 1913.

As chance had it, it was Nicholson who made the first comments in the Country Diary on the world transformed by the assassination in Sarajevo. Four months of convulsions that saw the German army just fail to carry out its long-rehearsed plan to reach Paris by December had shaken even the column's little world. The sheer weight of news and comment saw it driven out of the *Guardian* for the first time; between the declaration of war on August 4 and the end of 1914, it disappeared altogether from its usual place on the back page. There was thus no shortage of issues when Scott got in touch with Coward and Nicholson just before the new year, to ask if despatches from the countryside could resume. So far as possible, the column was to be a relief from the conflict, a policy passed on to new writers such as the prominent suffragette Helena Swanwick and the literary critic Basil de Selincourt, who joined the diary team in the following two years. But it was to prove impossible to avoid mention of the sweeping changes that world war brought to the settled rural world, described almost 90 years later to one of today's Country Diarists, John Vallins.

The old ways

℘ SEPTEMBER 2002 ☙

Last week, the one person I know who was born and bred in the village showed me an elaborately inscribed document dated January 28 1908, the form of indenture whereby his father, the son of a sawyer, was bound to 'put himself apprentice' to a blacksmith, 'to learn his art, trade or business' and 'faithfully to serve his secrets'. His pay was to rise, over four years, from 2s/6d to 5s/6d a week.

Recollections of that apprentice's later life, after the war in which he served and his brother was killed, make windows into a local life in which people went on foot, where horsepower and steampower were still important, and the rhythm of the farming year informed the pattern of daily life. The story goes that on one fortunate day he asked a girl who was walking by to hold the head of a horse he was shoeing, and thus began an acquaintance with the gamekeeper's daughter, which duly ripened into romance and marriage. Later, he worked on the railway as a platelayer. He was a big, strong man, well equipped for the heavy work involved, and became a 'ganger' or foreman.

At haymaking times, when the men got home in the evening, they would set to with wooden rakes and pitchforks as the rick was expertly built and thatched by hand. Such work was unpaid, but the children fetched and carried jugs of drink, and they had rides on the wagons or even on the slatted elevator that sloped up to the top of the rick. Now, a generation later, convoys of giant, gleaming tractors from regional contractors rumble along the lanes with machinery that makes short work of whole prairies of grass at the touch of a lever.

John Vallins

A new world

ဢ JANUARY 1915 ᙅ

New Year's Day has never in our generation brought with it to those who live a country life such novel conditions. The necessities of war have taken from us most, if not all, our able workers on the land; in many cases every man in the district of military age has gone. But the harvest has been got in and good work done during the autumn, old men, women and boys turning to with a will. The consequence is that I found, in visiting the best farm lands in south Lancashire and Cheshire during the past few days, that the preparation of the land is well forward. A considerable acreage has been sown with autumn wheat, and in many places the blade is well up and gives good promise for the coming season.

We had an almost unprecedented continuance of genial autumn weather, and it was only in late November that frost at last warned us that winter would come. All this has done much for the farmer and gardener, as it has been possible, even with restricted labour, to get along with the work. Cattle were out in the fields to a late date, which has been a great saving. The heavy rains that have followed and the recent rapid changes in temperature and weather seem to have been beneficial to the land, and the pastures during the past few days have looked wonderfully green and fresh. The agricultural outlook is one of good promise; all cattle, sheep, pigs and horses command a ready sale and satisfactory and advancing prices. The demand for milk is greater than ever, and farmer and gardener were never more likely to have a good sale for all they may be able to market during the coming season.

Arthur Nicholson

The recruits march off

ℬ FEBRUARY 1915 ℜ

The ploughman has been hard at work during the past few days, and the dryer and longer days have enabled him to make much better progress in preparing the seedbed: if wheat is to be drilled no time should be lost. The great anxiety is to have as large an acreage sown with this crop as possible in this wartime. Some are urging the farmer to sow beans, but in this district it has of late years not been a favourite crop. It is much more likely that there will be an increase in potato growing and in market garden farming, as far as this can be accomplished with the labour available. In many rural districts every man of military age has gone into the army and even the older men have taken service as drivers, either with the military or have come into the town as horse drivers. In this city alone many teams are idle and work at a standstill owing to the want of carters.

In passing through the country between the south-eastern suburbs of our city and the Derbyshire hills today, I found the grass everywhere in an unusually black state. We have not had a cold winter, but most of the land, where not covered with houses and works, is under grass, and owing to the continued rain for the past two months or more the great clouds of smoke, instead of drifting away and falling over a wide area miles in extent, have been precipitated by the rain and have obliterated all the show of green we are accustomed to see on the meadows in rural Cheshire and south-west Lancashire.

Arthur Nicholson

No one for hire

ⅎ FEBRUARY 1915 K

In Cumberland and in the northern counties generally, as also in Scotland, the hiring fairs are now over, and in several where, from time immemorial, it has always been possible to meet with able and expert farm servants if you were prepared to pay the market price, none was present. Many of the men have enlisted, and the few who remain at farm work had been re-engaged and did not trouble to attend. In other places a few put in an appearance, but prices asked were very high, and many farmers attended the second fair, still without engaging any help. The supply of women servants, old and young, was also very small and prices high.

In the past week we have had some extraordinary changes of temperature, but rather less rain, so by dint of working continuously from dawn to dark some more ploughing has been accomplished; but there are many fields that are so waterlogged that they must be left for a time.

On Saturday some species of gnats and small flies were on the wing in clouds, and when a shower came must have been dashed to the ground and would, no doubt, provide ample food for small birds, which in our district are unusually numerous. There has been very little frost this winter, and consequently birds have never wanted for a good supply of water, the absence of which in the case of many of our small species is a fatal trouble to them. Every bird-lover ought to have a large shallow bowl of water with a big stone in the middle always in the garden ready for them, and he will soon find how necessary it is to all birds. Cats, dogs, mice, rats and other animals will also pay it a visit if they can get at it.

Arthur Nicholson

Keepers' call-up

ജ JANUARY 2000 രജ

It seems probable that by the end of the 18th century the red squirrel was extinct in Scotland because of woodland clearance and severe winters. A number of reintroductions took place, one of which was in the Highlands on the Beaufort estate, a few miles west of Inverness. This was the only reintroduction north of the Great Glen and it took place in 1844 at the instigation of a Lady Lovat.

The squirrels rapidly spread along the wooded sides of the glens and straths until in 1890 they had reached Caithness in the north; by 1896 they were down to Ardnamurchan in the south-west. They did so much damage to woodland that they began to be killed in large numbers.

However, the damage continued and this led to the formation of the Highland Squirrel Club, which lasted from 1903 to 1946. The annual statements of this club were recently given to the archivist in Inverness and when I analysed them there were certainly some surprises.

In the first few years there were a total of 47 estates on the list in the counties of Ross-shire, Inverness-shire and Sutherland and the incentive to kill the squirrels was a 'bonus' of 3d a tail that rose in later years to 6d a tail. During the time of the club, an incredible 102,900 red squirrels were killed, with the maximum year being 1909 when 7,199 were killed. In 1907 there were 6,628 killed by shooting, trapping and poisoning.

A graph indicating numbers throughout the year has a marked dip in each of the two world wars because so many foresters/keepers were called up. Ironically, some of the highest numbers of squirrels killed each year were from the Beaufort estate, while the lowest was from Farr (which is our nearest estate) and it is interesting that red squirrels are still on both these areas.

The minutes of the annual meeting are virtually confined to squirrel business, but in the first world war estates were asked to collect, because of the country's food shortages, as many gulls' eggs as they could and take them to the nearest egg collecting depot, who should be urged to send them to the nearest military hospital free of charge.

Ray Collier

Wildlife and war

ℰ May 1915 ℭ

The question how far the changes in the habits of men this year will affect those of animals and birds naturally presents itself. Our disposition probably is to exaggerate the amount of disturbance likely to be caused. Migrating birds would no doubt avoid a battle, but they would flit over entrenched lines or even along them, were that necessary, unnoticing and unnoticed. Birds accustomed to human habitation do not need buildings in good repair and ruined villages will house swifts, swallows and martins as happily as if nothing were amiss. Shyer varieties will often find their haunts pre-occupied, but in compensation the countryside in general will be quieter; there seems little reason to suppose that many French or Belgian birds will come as far as England. In this country disturbance will occur chiefly in the neighbourhood of army camps; the inhabitants of downs and commons and those that nest in the furze will be aware of unusual bustle in their familiar haunts, even when their breeding sites have not been cleared away to make room for tents or huts. Thus a good many will have to put up with conditions or localities they prefer to avoid. The stonechat has already been seen twice in this part of Oxfordshire, though we have little land suitable for it and it has only once been recorded as breeding here. We shall look out also for the wheatear, a bird confined as a rule to our higher slopes, and even then seen only occasionally.

I must thank 'Oxoniensis' for his note on the cuckoo. From him I learn that north-east Oxon heard it three days before north-west – ie as early as Saturday, April 24.

Basil de Selincourt

Owls in the blackout

❧ FEBRUARY 1916 ☙

I am inclined to repeat a question asked by a Keswick correspondent: 'Is there anything funny about the owls just now?' We can hardly imagine that they object to lighting blackout orders, but certainly they appear to have taken a fancy for daylight hunting. The Keswick correspondent reports two different barn owls out in the morning and afternoon several times during the past two months, and also that a Sussex friend tells him that tawny owls 'are out hunting all over the place by three in the afternoon'. On the same date he wrote

Silent hunter; a barn owl seeking prey by day

to me, another correspondent reported that he saw a barn owl a few days ago in search of food near Nantwich a little before noon. Short-eared owls frequently hunt in the daytime but barn and tawny owls are habitually crepuscular and, at most seasons of the year, only fly in the daytime when accidentally disturbed. When, however, barn owls have hungry families demanding constant attention, they will sometimes strive to provide for them in broad daylight; only under these circumstances have I seen barn owls seeking prey by day. Although owls are early breeders we can hardly imagine that so many birds and in such widely separated places have already got young, and the conclusion is that there *is* something funny about them. The war, so far as one can guess, has not made the capture of mice or slumbering sparrows more difficult.

Thomas Coward

Women wanted

ଚ MARCH 1916 ଓ

The bleak winds of March, and snow falling in intermittent showers, tell us that the chill of winter is still upon us, but fortunately for those who have to travel in town or country the snow is thawing as it falls and in this district we have had no trouble with frosts. But we had difficulties enough in country places this week, owing to the intense darkness on Tuesday, Wednesday and Thursday evenings, as all was very overcast. Those who had to venture on the roads on foot after sundown found their journey alarming and dangerous, for motors rush by at rapid pace and the momentary bright light in the blackout rendered the darkness afterwards still more intense. Starlit nights have followed, fortunately, and the mantle of snow that covered the ground last night helped the traveller to make his way in safety.

The efforts to give an opportunity for women who are willing to help in the work of the farmer and other occupations on the land are multiplying, and it is to be hoped that many of the fairer sex will come forward, for if the farmers cannot secure help in place of the men who have joined the colours, it will be impossible to keep up the food supply. A spell of country life and fresh air will bring health and happiness, and much of the work is well within a woman's powers.

Arthur Nicholson

Mobilise the gardeners

ଚ APRIL 1916 ଓ

Each week. numbers of the men engaged on the land in this district are joining the colours, and it is now becoming most difficult to carry on ordinary farming. If the market gardens and small, highly cultivated holdings that are so numerous in south Lancashire and north Cheshire are to continue to produce even what they have done in recent years, some prompt effort must be made to get women to volunteer for the work. Already an appeal is being made for the better cultivation of small gardens and private holdings by cooperation, and there is ample work for the willing assistants in this, as in general agriculture. Those who look around them and see the rapid advance of spring must feel the necessity of a prompt answer to this national call, and will volunteer their service.

The beautiful weather of the last week has produced a marvellous change in field, garden and woodland. The hedgerows are green, and many spring flowers are blooming. The damson blossom is just beginning to show, and by Easter will be in perfection should the sunny weather continue. The almond trees are coming into flower, and I noticed this morning the rapid change that is taking place in all fruit buds in the orchard. The white rock rose, though it began early to show a few flowers, has never in my recollection bloomed so miserably. There has been a slight change for the better this week, but I fear this year's flowering is past recovery. Few bees are now being kept in our neighbourhood owing to fear of Isle of White disease. So we shall not feel the need of the white rock as we should if the honey-gatherers were about.

Arthur Nicholson

A soldier misbehaves

❧ MAY 1916 ☙

I learn from a Southport correspondent that a few days ago a crack shot in the national reserve shot a pair of dotterel out of a group of seven on the shore between Southport and Preston. Parties or 'trips' of dotterel still pass on migration along our Lancashire coast and a few pairs, very few, nest in the Lake District and on some of the Scottish mountains. The bird must not be confused with the ringed plover, often known as the ring dotterel, which nests upon the Lancashire beaches; it is a far rarer bird, and is quite rightly specially protected. But in spite of protection and the fact that it is now the close season, the law is openly defied, and, worse still, by a soldier. What is the use of county council orders and where are the police who are, in spite of the war, supposed to see that civil laws are obeyed?

For some strange reason, fly-fishers seem to think that at certain times or in certain places trout (or it may be salmon) will only rise to artificial flies made with dotterel feathers. I do not mind if I am offending the fly-fishing fraternity, and perhaps I am wrong in my ideas about these flies, but I do know that makers of flies use dotterel feathers, and that these two illegally slaughtered birds were given to a man in order that he might pluck their beautiful feathers from them and make them up into a lure for fish! The same gunner brought down a wood pigeon that had in its crop no fewer than 553 grains of barley; there the man was doing good and breaking no law. What a pity that he could not confide his attention to the harmful wood-pigeons which, by the way, are much more difficult to shoot than confiding migrant dotterels!

Thomas Coward

Wartime fertiliser

₭ November 1996 ℞

Bedraggled Old Man's Beard, caught up in hawthorn berries and rotting purple bullaces, festoons trees in the derelict orchard and is rampant in hedgebanks above a dripping slate-cutting along the sunken lane to Halton quay. On the quay, high tide has left reed stems, wood and seaweed, swirled to the foot of old lime kilns. These distinctive buildings, with massive walls and broad archways leading to gleaming, lime-encrusted caverns, were last used in 1916. Then, burnt lump-lime was discharged from the arches, loaded into wagons and hauled up the hill to Viverdon Down to sweeten or neutralise acid soils, ploughed as part of the war effort. Most Tamar valley kilns were built in the late 18th and early 19th centuries, before the widespread use of artificial and chemical manures. Plymouth 'marble' and South Wales coal were brought upriver in barges, winched out of holds, manhandled ashore and lugged up steep ramps to the kiln tops, often by packhorse, and, at Halton quay, in trucks pulled by a wire rope worked by water wheel. Alternate layers of coal and limestone were packed down into the kiln wells, some more than 6m deep, to be fired and kept alight by skilled lime-burners. One tonne of stone produced 11cwts of lime after eight hours burning and Halton's four kilns easily produced 500-600 tonnes a year, sold at 13s6d a tonne in the second half of last century, to be spread over fields, and market gardens in St Mellion and St Dominic. Now, limestone is pulverised by powerful machinery in Dorset quarries and brought long distances in huge lorries. This afternoon, the quay's quiet is enjoyed by a few people in parked cars, gazing at calm reflections of Devon fields and glassy, golden water, studded with leaves, flooding upstream through the great meander beneath Pentillie's woods.

Virginia Spiers

Where are the women?

‿ MAY 1916 ℞

The wet, dull weather is depressing, but the temperature in this district has not fallen much and our corn crops look well. It is said among north-country folk that 'who views his oats in May goes weeping away', but I have passed by some today that ought not to depress anyone. The grass is coming on well and on my way through the meadow each morning, I can note its rapid full growth. It will now hide a corncrake or a partridge, and should we have some sunny weather, it will come on apace.

Great efforts are being made to get in the potatoes but labour is hard to find, for though this is work that women can do, their labour is in such demand that I know many farmers who are willing to give a good wage and yet can get no help. Matters grow worse each week, and the country districts are becoming rapidly denuded of the working population, from which agriculture must inevitably suffer.

Sheep-shearing has now begun in southern counties, though it will be some eight to ten weeks before all the fleeces are off amongst the flocks in the mountain districts. All agree it is a good prospect for the flockmasters. The season has been favourable in most parts of the country, and the price of wool is not unlikely to rise considerably.

Arthur Nicholson

Victims of the war

ஒ JUNE 1916 ஓ

'I came across six dead herons tied to a tree in the Goyt valley,' writes a friend of mine. Some of them were quite young, evidently not having left the nest, and all had been killed at about the same time. One reader of the *Manchester Guardian*, if he sees this note, will be especially annoyed; he has watched the birds here for years, even before he was certain that a small heronry had been established. Now some law-breaking keeper or water bailiff has apparently waited until the young birds were hatched to murder the whole brood; it was on the Cheshire side, and the heron is a protected bird in Cheshire. Much good protection seems to be! The sportsman, or the sportsman's agents, appear to care nothing about the law, unless a sportsman of another type, usually called a poacher, is the offender. The object of wild bird protection was to prove that wild birds were public or rather national property, but probably the excuse would be that it does not matter in wartime. Many of our finest sportsmen, however, have refused to preserve game during the war, but they, or at any rate some of them, observe the law and protect the scheduled birds. A note from another friend tells me of his discovery of the nest of a merlin on the Lancashire moors; it is to be hoped that no one will destroy the eggs or young of this interesting little falcon.

Thomas Coward

Children in the fields

&⁊ JUNE 1916 ☙

The weather in the south of Britain has improved during the past few days and on Sunday it felt at last like a summer day. But last night was wet again and it was difficult to realise early this morning that midsummer is at hand. As we travelled down to Lancashire, the gentle sunshine quickly altered the temperature and we began to see the mowing machine at work, but though we passed by fields where the hay seemed ready to cut, nowhere did we see anyone busy with it. On Sunday we had seen a party of women and children making and leading the hay in a large field on the south side of the Thames not seven miles from Westminster.

In journeying through the Midlands and on to Manchester, it was very evident that the cold weather and absence of sun had kept back the hay crop, as very little is yet got in, but the appearance of other crops is good. Oats, beans, turnips and potatoes are all doing well as far as I could tell; but I fear from what I hear in other districts that frost has done some mischief. I am glad to see that on some of the railway banks the hay has not been burnt and I sincerely hope that it will not be, for in such times as these it is a shameful waste to destroy it. If horses won't eat some of the worst of it, certainly donkey owners would be glad to pay something for it, and in the present difficulty with regard to haulage, the donkey is becoming a valuable assistant, not only in such great centres as London and Manchester but also to the farmer. Donkeys are much better cared for in all places than they were formerly and consequently are capable of doing much more work.

Thomas Coward

Bad for bedding plants
ᔕ JUNE 1916 ᔕ

Heavy thunderstorms have deluged most parts of this district during the past few days and last evening closed with such ominous darkness and heavy atmosphere that it was a surprise when I found this morning that our bit of ground was as hard and dry as a biscuit and the only moisture in the meadow grass as I walked through it was a light dew. It was not until the afternoon that a slight fall of rain came, so fortunately the weather has not spoiled the first day of the Royal Show. No one who takes an interest in any branch of agriculture should miss seeing this show, as it is in many ways one of the best ever held.

Where very little rain has fallen, and as we have also had little hot sunny weather, our hay has come on slowly and much in this district is still uncut. Our gardens are full of flowers, however. Many of the most beautiful varieties of rhododendron are now at their best, and peonies have been a wonderful show this season. At Kew and in the London parks, squares and private gardens, the lupins of many varieties have been laden with particularly fine blooms, as they have been in the gardens in this district.

Owing to the war we have seen little of bedding-out plants this season and in my view it is no loss. We have in our herbaceous plants the possibility of a far finer variety and succession of beautiful flowers for our summer season than is possible with the costly and troublesome bedding-out plants, whose length of life and beauty are so dependent on the absence of frost.

Arthur Nicholson

How about goats?

ଚ JULY 1916 ଔ

Today, like so many lately, has been showery but the temperature is higher. There has, however, been no sunshine or wind to dry the ground and foliage after the heavy rain that fell last night and early morning, and we are looking with some anxiety for haymaking weather. How we are to get in our hay crop is difficult to say, as labour is so scarce and there never was a time when it was so difficult to buy labour-saving machines suitable for agriculture.

We may congratulate ourselves in many ways on the success of the Royal Show. There has been no more interesting exhibition of animals for many years, if ever. The sheep and goats struck me as a particularly fine show, and both these animals are specially worth our notice at the present time. The needs of the nation demand that our stock of sheep should be increased, and suitable breeds be brought to the notice of flockmasters. It is anxiously hoped that the government will act liberally with regard to the price at which the wool clip is to be commandeered, for if only a bare price is given, many men, owing to the high price they have had to buy at, will be discouraged from keeping their sheep next season and far too many animals will go to the butcher. Goats are most useful, and could be kept largely at great advantage in a district like ours where the milk supply is always so needed.

Arthur Nicholson

Railway wastelands

℅ August 1916 ℭ

Each day the weather for harvesting has improved. Last night was clear and warm, and the slight mist and dew early this morning soon disappeared, and the hay was ready to turn and gather up. From what I have seen during the day the greater part of our hay crop in south Lancashire and Cheshire will be safe in stack or barn this evening. The continuing high temperature night and day has brought on the corn wonderfully, and this morning the first change of tint to yellow-green was on fields of both oats and wheat, and if this bright, sunny weather continues, we shall want every able and willing worker to help with the corn harvest.

Those who have been about the country recently and have noticed the extraordinary success of the allotments this season must look with keen regret at the increasing area of absolutely waste land in the hands of the railway and canal companies. Much of it could be cultivated profitably without inconvenience to their owners, but it seems to be no one's duty to see to these economies, though they are of national importance, and we must wait till some shareholders see that money can be made out of them. I passed by a place today where a railway company had allowed about an acre of land on one side of the line to be cultivated, and it carried heavy crops. Across the rails, a similar spot was growing weeds that even in these times no one will cut for any purpose.

Arthur Nicholson

Too few to help

❧ AUGUST 1916 ❧

What a change a week has wrought in the landscape! The dark green herbage in mountain and meadow gives good promise of plenty for our sheep and cattle, and the foliage on the trees and hedgerows, that was here and there showing a sign of the hot, dry time we had passed through, is now refreshed and the growth in the woodland is rejoicing the forester's heart. If timber is ever going to pay it ought to do now, for it has had a second year of unusual growth, and in some woods that I have examined the oaks and more valuable class of trees have done the best. There is land so suitable to the oak tree that it will come on as rapidly as a larch on its favourite soil and there are patches of this good oak-growing land on the estate of our Manchester Corporation in Cumberland. It is a curious fact that in the notes of a Manchester gentleman travelling through the Vale of St John and the Thirlmere district some 80 years ago, the fact of this rapid growth and perfection of the oak trees is mentioned.

The corn has come on now to near perfection and as the rain-storms get fewer more farmers will set to with their harvest. The shortage of labour is a serious difficulty, and in some cases queer teams of volunteers and others get to work. One afternoon last week a farmer's wife told me she had just milked 27 cows, a very small girl had managed a few, and an old hand and a friend who happened to call accounted for the rest. It was the weekly holiday in the neighbouring small town, and many young people had come as very willing and efficient helpers in the hay.

Arthur Nicholson

The squire's wife

℘ AUGUST 1916 ℘

Every opportunity when the weather is fine is being taken to make progress with the corn harvest in our district of south Lancashire and Cheshire, and a considerable part of the crop is in stook. What is wanted now is bright sunshine and a drying wind. Then we should soon have our harvest safely gathered in, for I cannot believe that the call of the farmers for help will not be cheerfully responded to by the men and women of all classes in our district. Not many weeks ago I saw the squire's wife in a country parish driving a milkcart, and this she does every day, wet or fine. Her good man is at the war, and all the younger men are with him, but the work is being done.

We may grumble, who want fine weather for getting in crops or for the family holiday-making, but certainly these storms of rain and gleams of sunshine have brought many of our garden plants to a wonderful growth, and in many cases to a perfection of bloom. At the present moment the long trailing tendrils of the jasmine are tipped with hundreds of white, star-like flowers shown to perfection on a mass of dark green foliage, and we have still many roses.

I have complaints from the mountain country of the Lake District of the depredation of foxes. So many of the active followers of the chase have recently left the countryside to take their places in the army that those who remain at home will have to stir themselves to great effort, or we shall have a bad time for poultry-keepers and for the shepherds next spring.

Arthur Nicholson

CHAPTER THREE

STRANGE HARVEST

It did not take long for the people of Britain to realise that the jaunty spirit of adventure that fired the first troops sent to France in 1914 was misplaced. By New Year's Day in 1916, the archaeologist Gertrude Bell was writing to her mother begging that there would never again be a year such as 1915. Later in the month, parliament passed the first Conscription Act, which was to send less eager soldiers to the trenches. The novelist DH Lawrence was on a winter weekend in a Cornish village where he jotted down the bleak comments of young women sewing buttons on to khaki army uniforms. 'Every stitch I put in goes through my heart,' one told him, with an eloquence that sounds suspiciously like the writer's own. But such feelings were increasingly shared.

Their tone was justified. The year developed into one of disasters and death on a previously unimaginable scale. Collapse in Turkey was followed by mutinies among Russian troops on the eastern front, where more than 1,500,000 soldiers had been taken prisoner by the German and Austrian armies. At Easter the Irish rebels launched their doomed but psychologically potent rising in Dublin. The western front was bogged down in stalemate, following the fearful losses of 1915, when chlorine gas made its debut on the battlefield and the opening British barrage at Neuve Chapelle saw more shells fired in three hours than during the whole of the Boer war. As the first conscripts began their brief training before sailing for France in February 1916, a still more terrible battle of attrition began at Verdun, a fortress that the French had sworn to hold and into which the Germans deliberately encouraged them to pour troops to be slaughtered.

The consequences are written on war memorials in almost every village in the United Kingdom as well as in memoirs such as Winston Churchill's graphic image of feeling, as he read the death toll, as if he was standing in the dark on a hillside, watching the lights of a great city go out one by one. Everyone had lost someone they knew, from farm cottagers to the prime minister, Herbert Asquith, whose son Lieutenant Raymond Asquith died with the Guards Division in September, during the long and largely unavailing battle of the Somme. To read the *Manchester Guardian*'s yellowing files from these months is still upsetting. Every day, a panel records the number of British troops killed in action; the officers' total always in the hundreds, the men's in the thousands. The Country Diary was surrounded by almost unbearable headlines such as 'Woman's ten sons lost in the war'.

In these circumstances, it was hardly surprising that one of the Country Diary team, Basil de Selincourt, sought anonymity by using the single initial 'S', explaining to the paper's editor, CP Scott, that in such catastrophic days, his friends in London and the arts world might think it 'a little trivial to be watching insects or enjoying the countryside'. Scott reassured him that it was vital that at least one part of the newspaper, however modest, maintained an interest in such lasting things; day after day, the Country Diary avoided the war altogether, sometimes the only part of the paper's eight pages to do so. Helena Swanwick, although a gutsy suffragette, was particularly determined to concentrate on flowers at Kew and in her own garden nearby, to remind depressed or bereaved readers of the year's cycle – death in winter followed by rebirth in spring – and the prospect, as she hoped, of better things to come.

The exceptions came largely when Arthur Nicholson took the farmers' part on a range of issues, joined from time to time by the other diarists when the subject was the dominant one of the shortage of manpower in the fields. As might be expected from a radical paper, the *Manchester Guardian* welcomed the new responsibilities that war work gave to women; always a keen supporter of the suffrage movement, Scott corresponded early on with Swanwick about the possible political rewards when the war was won and the women's part in victory too obvious to be overlooked, a view in tune with his readers. At the very beginning of the war, when the diary was suspended, a retired senior inspector of schools, Mary Mason, wrote tartly to the *Guardian* complaining that 'in some places women are working in the harvest, but it does not seem to have occurred to them generally. Shame.'

Not everyone agreed. In 1915 *Country Life* ran a sceptical editorial headed 'The Women Difficulty in Agriculture', suggesting that life in the fields was just too much for volunteers from country houses or the towns. The writer argued: 'The woman of the fields is accustomed to use language not familiar to polite ears, and the ears of the refined students have often been considerably shocked. The two classes cannot work together.' Some counties, such as Hampshire, avoided trouble by insisting on a preliminary programme of training, but there were protests and demands for extra wages from the traditional corps of migrant women workers, tough, Gypsy-like freelances who moved round the country according to the picking seasons for different crops and feared that the volunteers were stealing their jobs.

In fact, as Arthur Nicholson repeatedly argued, there was more than enough work to go round, as the battlefields demanded ever increasing numbers of men, and age ranges for conscription were progressively raised. One of the *Guardian*'s major campaigns during the conflict was against the temporary suspension of compulsory education during harvest – a measure taken in 1915 by 20 rural county councils – so that children could take the place of farmworkers who had gone to fight. The tight-fistedness of employers fired the paper's support for a better-paid system of employing farm labourers generally. Petty acts of meanness, such as the refusal to pay even token pocket-money to school volunteers on Holiday Harvest Camps for Boys, helped to secure the establishment of the Agricultural Wages Board in 1917.

There were also controversies about the best use of land, incentives to put neglected areas to agricultural use and the right choice of crops to meet the needs of the wartime economy. In 1917, the blockade by German submarines was taking such a toll of allied shipping that Country Diary writers were prepared to sanction almost anywhere being tilled for wheat, oats or barley. That year and in 1918, more than 1,200,000 new hectares were brought under plough.

And of course, there was the shattered world of the western front. Like almost everyone else, the diary writers had friends in the trenches as well as naturalist contacts who sent back notes on the way that birds and plants were somehow surviving Armageddon. One letter to Thomas Coward from Gallipoli described how 'clumsy corn buntings perch on the trench wire here,' and reported turtledoves skimming between shellbursts. Another, sent only six weeks before the end of the war, reports that 'linnets and wheatears are singing near the graves of Lancashire fusiliers and men of the Manchester Regiment.'

Most poignantly, a detachment of snipers filed a list of birds which they could see or hear from their position in a derelict barn 'somewhere in Flanders', as the official argot had it, when the names and positions of units could not be revealed in case it helped the Germans. Between firing at the opposite trenches, the men noted a moorhens' nest on the abandoned farm pond, the safe hatching of the birds' eggs and the groggy debut of the fledglings between the opposing armies' lines. They saved a blackbird's nest from a hayrick that German shelling set on fire but watched, unable to intervene, while the more cruel side of nature was played out. A little owl based in the ruined farm's orchard regularly hunted for fledglings, returning to her young with a baby blackbird or thrush in her talons. The supreme moment came when soft, liquid snatches of birdsong revealed the presence of a golden oriole. Spying it from their dangerous loopholes in a roofless barn, the snipers were at one with Helena Swanwick who, as Thomas Coward reports below, was watching the same glorious species – much rarer in Britain – from a Cornish clifftop.

Keeping the kindling

❧ JANUARY 1917 ❧

At daybreak this morning there seemed to be indications – which unfortunately were not fulfilled later – that the mild, damp weather of yesterday would give place to a clear, sunny, winter atmosphere, which might do something to dry the land and give us a chance of getting to work on it. We were early out in both garden and field planning what could best be accomplished pending an improved condition of the soil, so much desired, and soon found plenty of heavy tasks before us.

There are few places in the country where economy in firing cannot be achieved by the gathering up of waste wood that is lying about. If it is not used for fuel, much of it will be of no value for that or any other purpose a few months hence. The ash from this and all other vegetable matter burned should be applied to the land, as it is one of our most valuable fertilisers.

Motor-ploughing is, I am glad to say, being tried in many counties, the necessary capital being found by public-spirited landlords and others. It is virtually the only way in which the difficulty of want of skilled labour can be got over in many districts. Now we may hope to see a large acreage sown with oats in the coming spring and it is earnestly to be hoped that there may be a good season for this and our other crops.

Arthur Nicholson

Owls in the trenches

ဢ JANUARY 1917 ႒

Several correspondents in France have referred to the owls that find the trenches such profitable mouseries that they hunt by day. The latest note on the subject comes from one of our south coast camps where a light brown owl – probably a barn owl – found daylight sport anything but peaceful. The lads who were watching it were not the trouble, but a number of gulls resented its presence 'and flew excitedly round it', though apparently they did not venture to attack the unusual-looking bird. Then a rook, no doubt attracted by the calls of the gulls, came along, flying above the owl. It darted upon the mouse-hunter, striking it on the back with its beak, and down fell the owl. 'We saw it no more,' writes my correspondent, but it does not follow that the owl was slain; a rook coming down with wings half-closed, 'stooping' like a falcon, is certainly a formidable foe, but the feathers on an owl's back are wonderfully thick and soft and would act as an elastic cushion, protecting the body.

A small bird, which 'seems to fly in jumps' has puzzled the same correspondent; it is black and white with a 'black boomerang band on its white throat' and white streaks – outer feathers – on the tail. Undoubtedly our friend the pied wagtail; many of these birds are now wintering on our southern shores.

Thomas Coward

A break from the war

℘ JANUARY 1917 ℧

'Do mice eat cockroaches?' asks a correspondent. In his home were many of these annoying insect pests popularly but erroneously called 'black beetles' (they are neither black not beetles), but when another pest in the form of a mouse turned up, most of the cockroaches vanished. Remains of the insects – the hard skins or shells with the contents cleaned out – were found lying about, suggesting that the mice had dined. Our common house mouse is decidedly omnivorous, as many of us know to our cost. In my house I have known it eat the bodies of large noctuid moths that had fallen, singed, beneath a gas burner, but I have no recollection of hearing of it feeding on cockroaches. These insects do not look attractive as food, specially when we find them baked in a loaf, but some birds and lizards seem to enjoy them. Bats will eat them if hungry, but they prefer moths or beetles. I have tried both the noctule and greater horseshoe bat with them. Cockroaches, though they run swiftly, make no fight for life when seized by a bat; all bats, even the smaller ones, appear to enjoy a struggle with their victim. The cockroach gives in at once. Field mice will eat them, and indeed all our smaller rodents, from the rat to the tiny harvest mouse, enjoy an insect diet for a change; the gnawing teeth, suited to a vegetarian, are often stained with the life juices of insects and sometimes with the red blood of birds or mammals, even of their own relatives.

Thomas Coward

Daylight for digging

&O JANUARY 1917 C&

Yesterday the weather was still bitterly cold and a snowfall threatened many times, yet we felt it was an improvement on the damp, dark days we had before Christmas. This morning, however, it was clear and fine at dawn, and we have had many bursts of sunshine, although I doubt if the temperature has been much over freezing point. It is still very difficult to make any headway with the cultivation of gardens and fields. Those who have taken up cultivation of plots of rough ground have had very bad conditions and weather for their start, but I hope the authorities will this year make the daylight change not later than April 1. This would help all who have a garden to get early to work on their plots, and now – knowing that we cannot hope for help from our old day-men – we shall tackle the work ourselves. Here and there women are taking up this business in suburban gardens and find it pays them well. It is a great pity more do not help in this way, for there is no doubt a very large area of ground in the gardens of private houses went out of cultivation last year. Our determination should be not only that this land shall be used but also that it shall be put under intensive culture.

I noticed that one of the authorities speaking on agriculture appealed for help in the destruction of rabbits, pheasants and sparrows, and also of mice and rats, but he seemed to have omitted the hare. As perhaps our chief object now is to protect wheat, one must denounce 'this modest animal' as one of its greatest enemies. Even where hares are not very abundant, they seem to have a wonderful way of finding the wheatfield when the stem of the wheat is just at its full growth and the taste of it sweet and just to their liking. Then woe betide the farmer unless he can get a friendly sportsman to come along. We in Lancashire and Cheshire know of districts where, on account of the depredations of hares, it is not worthwhile to grow wheat. On one estate where there is no shooting I have counted 40 hares on a field of little more than two acres.

Arthur Nicholson

Pheasants on the prowl

ᔕ FEBRUARY 1917 ᘒ

A cock pheasant, a correspondent reports, was disturbed a few days ago in Manchester Road, Withington. The news suggests that hard weather and lack of convenient food may account for its somewhat unusual wanderings. Very likely, though, during these days of shortage, pheasants may be expected to wander even nearer to the city than this. On many estates no birds were reared in spring 1916, but the carefully tended pheasants refused to become extinct. Not only have they survived, but they have also given the lie to those who declared that they were bad parents by raising their own broods of healthy and vigorous youngsters. These really wild young pheasants are more likely to wander in search of feeding grounds than the semi-domestic birds whose estate mothers were fussy hens whose food, specially prepared, was always ready for them in appropriate places. When the sportsman once more raises his gun at these feathered targets, he may find that bringing down these hardy birds requires more skill than was the case in prewar days.

The food problem is affecting other birds than pheasants but in these parts birds are facing the difficulties together. In one stubble field, feeding together in a flock, were no fewer than 20 different species, possibly more, for I saw them all clearly as they hopped and fluttered on the grass: fieldfares and redwings happily joined by finches and buntings, chaffinches especially and yellowhammers, and joining them a little party of great, coal and blue tits, all of them gleaning the scattered husks. The tits especially were dining on the seeds of the many weeds that infested the corn. When animal food is scarce, insectivorous birds will take to seed-eating. Come the spring, when the small creatures start getting abundant, the hard-billed finches will return to an animal diet of caterpillars and other grubs.

Thomas Coward

The Food Controller

❧ MARCH 1917 ❧

How the earwigs, beetle larvae and earthworms must hate the Food Controller! When, quite in the fashion, I was breaking up some fresh ground in my small garden, I caused great annoyance and considerable injury to numerous worms and insects, which no doubt thought that they were safe in winter quarters. It was the earwigs that I especially noticed, and I was almost sorry for them, for, like birds, they were sitting on their eggs. I had to stop occasionally to watch a half-awake mother earwig, if I did not happen to have damaged her with my spade. She turned up an expostulating and threatening tail, metaphorically rubbed her eyes, dazzled by the unexpected light, and then began to fuss around, striving to gather together those precious eggs. She is a model mother among insects, and when the tiny larvae – very like her in general appearance – are hatched, she looks after them in quite a correct manner, while the babes seem to recognise their nurse and crowd round her like much more highly developed animals, even crawling upon her back for a ride. The earwig is not popular but she has some excellent points, and the really neat arrangement of her beautiful wings, folding like a fan from the centre of their forward edge so that they will tuck safely inside her short wingcase, is most wonderful.

Thomas Coward

Patriotic trenching

ℬ April 1917 ℛ

My pen was guilty of telescoping two ideas in the little record published last Wednesday. My head was full of the dark crimson blossoms of the elm, and I was intending to write of them, but found my space gone in a preliminary note on the patch of crocuses so cleverly set under the beeches near the rhododendron dell. I knew they were beeches and wrote of their 'silver' stems; but I see now, staring me in the face, that I must have written 'elm boles'. My fault! But no one could call elm boles silver in any light. Sometimes they look a velvety black; sometimes, in bright sunshine, like Havana-coloured corduroy; but never, no never, anything like silver, unless, indeed silver that had not been cleaned for a year.

A gentleman whose patriotic trenching was being held up by the snow, recently comforted himself with the assurance that, anyhow, 'snow is a grand manure.' This is perhaps a rather strong statement, and most of us would be willing to forfeit any small nourishment there may be in snow for the sake of getting a friable soil for seed-sowing and some warmth to welcome young plants. Snow may get some chemical properties from the atmosphere through which it passes; some people recognise the 'sooty smell' of snow. In mid-winter it is a most valuable blanket, and beneath it many processes go on. But in mid-April we would prefer the blanket to be removed, and the sun to get to business.

Helena Swanwick

Transport needed

ᔕ April 1917 ᔕ

The country in the Midlands yesterday had a dreary, sodden appearance, and the higher lands on the borders of Cheshire, Bedfordshire and Derbyshire were covered with snow. Rain fell in our own district during the night, and the bitterly cold north wind this morning, though it helped to dry the soil to some extent, gave little hope of genial spring weather. The first primroses are out and a polyanthus gave them the lead a fortnight earlier, but our spring flowers are late – even the daisy has only put out one bloom on half an acre of lawn.

It is bitterly disappointing to the farmers, anxious as they are to respond to the call to produce wheat, that there has been scarcely a chance in our district to sow any this spring, owing to the weather. Now they are hoping to achieve some success by drilling oats and barley, but much must depend upon the weather. In most districts of Lancashire and Cheshire, potatoes have for years been grown largely, and there is little doubt that the present shortage will lead to a great effort to increase the acreage under this crop and in gardens and smallholdings a very large area is being planted with them. Go where you will in suburban and country districts, you will find land being cultivated that has either been waste for years or had little or no attention. One hopes that before the time comes for the distribution of the produce there will be some effort made to create market facilities, so that it can be disposed of. In the past quantities of fruit and vegetables have been wasted, as there was no means of profitably marketing them. Want of arrangement and carriage have been the trouble.

Arthur Nicholson

The golden oriole

ℬ MAY 1917 ℰ

My colleague 'HMS' has had one of those treats that fall to the lot of but few of us – a good view of a male golden oriole, one of the most brilliant of the rare birds that visit our islands from time to time. She was sitting at the edge of a Cornish cliff with a friend when the bird passed below, and at once its orange and black plumage caught her attention. The description she sends could apply to no other bird. The golden oriole might be a regular summer visitor to England, especially to the southern and western counties, but it is seldom allowed a chance to nest. How pleasant it is to record the bird's presence without the words 'shot', 'trapped', or 'killed'.

A black tern, an adult bird in sooty plumage, was beating up and down over the waters of Redesmere a few evenings ago. Every few moments, it turned sharply and dived towards the surface, but without the headlong dash of its more maritime congeners; indeed, it always checked its pace before striking the water, for this bird is almost entirely an insect feeder, and was swooping to nip up some gnat or fly that was on the wing. The black tern is now a passing visitor only, but before modern drainage it nested plentifully in Britain, especially in Norfolk, Lincolnshire and Yorkshire.

Thomas Coward

Peaceful interlude

ஐ JUNE 1917 ଔ

'Don't go up there, children; there's nothing there!' So called the tired woman, but the children knew better. With a reproachful 'But mother … ' they tripped up the shallow, irregular steps in the miniature limestone ravine, where the more precious encrusted saxifrages were pouring forth their honeyed perfume in the sunshine from countless white panicles and plumes. One did so wish that these children could be alone here for a while. This was the place of their inexpressible dreams. One child stood absolutely still and just touched a spray with a gentle forefinger, adoring it with big eyes. She was silent quite a while and then breathed, in a kind of ecstatic moan: 'Oh! And the little trees!' as if she were recognising a country that was her home. These were the pygmy junipers that stand among the rocks, not more than a third the height of the tallest saxifrage. Another child discovered that the lovely smell came from the flowers, and she was not satisfied until she had sniffed at all within her reach. She was more active in her body, and jumped up and down the steps and shouted each discovery; the *Raimondia* in the crannies particularly rejoiced her. But the silent one stood as if remembering, and God knows what recognition lay in her eyes.

Helena Swanwick

Shoot the rooks

᎒ JUNE 1917 Ꮣ

The face of the country has changed wonderfully during the past week. Especially is this noticeable in such districts as that between Leicester and London, where for miles you pass through grassland, acres of which are now a sheet of yellow or crimson, for never have I seen the buttercups or clover in more perfect bloom. As I passed through my own meadow this morning the clover was so abundant that it was difficult to believe that it had not been ploughed for years, and a few seasons ago there was no clover to be seen in it. Even entirely neglected grass fields are growing some fine herbage this summer. The crops are still coming forward well, for since the rain ceased we have had a succession of hot, sunny days and heavy dew at night.

I see that again complaints are being made of damage to farm crops by rabbits, but surely this is the farmer's own fault. In these tight times, farmers should see that their crops are not injured, and that both hares and rabbits, particularly rabbits, which can never pay for keeping on agricultural land, are properly dealt with. I hope all who are near rookeries have been careful to shoot a good proportion of the young birds, or we shall have a heavy loss to face in what we all hope is to be a great potato crop this autumn. Already I have spotted rooks doing some mischief.

Arthur Nicholson

No, hold your fire

᎒ JUNE 1917 Ꮣ

Growers of fruit and vegetables, whether amateur or professional, are overlooking the fact that increased production is certain to bring increased difficulties; the more plants we grow, the more insects and other animal pests we find are feeding on them. If the protection of our food supply was less urgent, the sudden interest in economic biology would be almost amusing; why did gardeners, farmers and ratepayers not pay attention in the past to scientific cultivation? Some of them did not realise that we had a Board of Agriculture, and few troubled to ask its advice or study its literature. Now that their plants are coming up and showing the effects of the ravages of pests, when, too, in many cases it is too late to remedy the problem, they are trying to throw the blame on others. Ground requires preparation and crops need watching and guarding, but we are foolish if we listen to the order or warning to keep down or destroy this or that creature unless we are sure that we know what it is that we are fighting and how it is injuring us. We hear much about the fly danger, but how many of those who are told to 'Kill that fly' know the difference between the common housefly and the dipterous parasites that destroy the caterpillars of the cabbage butterfly and other food-destroying insects? How many, again, know the useful hoverflies or the many other insects that feed on insects? We were asked to destroy sparrows, and already hear of the eggs of insectivorous birds having been brought in by children. We may well have insect plagues.

I fear that I cannot help the Urmston correspondent whose apple-twig is attached. The small insects in the curled and withered leaves are probably aphids and leaf-rolling caterpillars. The trees should have been sprayed with some insecticide before the pests got a hold. It by no means follows, however, that the fruit crop will be seriously affected. I should advise my correspondent to look at the Board of Agriculture leaflets on apple culture and aphids. It may show how to guard against a resurgence of trouble.

Thomas Coward

A new race of farmers?

ℰℴ AUGUST 1917 ℭℛ

In many parts of this district we had a heavy thundershower on Sunday evening, and it left the grass very wet yesterday. Though there was no further rainfall during the day, there was a heavy dew last night, and I had a wet walk through the meadow grass this morning. We have nothing to complain about in this district with regard to weather, as with the refreshing rainfalls has come a rise in the temperature, and again we have had a good growing time for vegetables and fruit crops. The grass is coming on quickly, and as far as I have seen the corn crops have had no setback.

It seems a pity to many who know the work and patience required to get into satisfactory cultivation meadow and pasture lands that they should be ploughed up to plant corn. I have passed by thousands of acres during the plast six months in various parts of the country that are only half-cultivated – one may indeed say really neglected land that has in the past been under corn. Why not spend the time and money on that, so that when the war is over these acres will be ready for the new race of farmers whom we hope to see improving the land culture of the mother country?

Arthur Nicholson

Crusade against rats

ℰℴ SEPTEMBER 1917 ℭℛ

The steady barometer, now at a fair height, has meant, as we expected, fine weather, which has enabled the farmers to get in their corn. In this district to a very large extent it is now safely in stack or barn, and what there is to lead will, we hope, in a few days be gathered in. Once more, I return to the old subject and ask why, now we have got our grain, we do not better protect it from the ravages of rats and other vermin? A large percentage of the food of the country is lost in this way, and if we saved even a part of this loss, by a crusade against rats, the chief offenders, it would make a valuable addition to our supplies. The effort, to be successful, must be a national one, but there is no doubt that an appeal from authority would meet with a ready response.

In all parts of the country I have visited, I have found the corn in a much better state now that it is gathered in than seemed likely during the wet stormy weather of August, and accounts from other districts in many counties of the north and south are reassuring. Everywhere there is an exceptionally fine crop of roots. The grass on pasture and fellside is so abundant and in many cases of such fine quality, unusually rich in clover this autumn, that it seems difficult to imagine there is any necessity to put up the price of milk.

Arthur Nicholson

Butterflies on the western front

ஐ SEPTEMBER 1917 ଔ

Already a peacock butterfly has selected our curtains for winter quarters, but it is early for this fly to be going into hibernation, and many are still on the wing, settling on the scabious and ragworts in the lanes or the flowers in our gardens. Perhaps the yellowing foliage of the sycamore and showers of curled, crisp beech leaves already down had given it a warning; it had a duty to fulfil: a long death-like slumber and a short flight next spring to find the young nettles and lay its eggs, thus linking up the years. It is many years since peacocks and red admirals were so abundant as they are now; everywhere people are struck by the numbers, not only locally nor even just in other parts of England. A friend in France writes: 'The crops here are barbed wire, thistles and nettles; I don't know what the first produces, but the two last have brought out great lots of painted ladies, red admirals, peacocks, and a positive swarm of small tortoise-shells.' The weeds of the war-scarred, untilled land have produced one beautiful crop.

Another and rarer insect that is about is the big convolvulus hawk moth. I hear of its occurrence recently at Sale and yesterday the corpse of one in a toffee-box reached me by post. The sender gave neither his name nor any particulars of locality; would he kindly let me have them? This moth is exceedingly irregular in its appearance, and is undoubtedly an immigrant, so that all records are of interest.

Thomas Coward

Fish rations

ɞ SEPTEMBER 1917 ᗉ

Though the Food Controller may consider that the supply of fresh-water fish is not of great importance, the cormorants evidently hold a different opinion. There were two busily sampling what they could catch on one of the Delamere meres; they thought a big, lazy bream well worth diving for. Was it this idea that attracted a passing shag – the smaller and much rarer green cormorant – to see what it could find on the canal near Mossley? Probably it was either lost or fagged out when migrating, for it allowed itself to be caught, and when I last heard of it, three days ago, was thriving well in captivity. The big cormorant often wanders inland for a little fishing, but the shag is seldom met with far from the sea.

Another convolvulus hawk moth has been captured locally. A correspondent writes that he caught one hovering over his nicotiana flowers at Prestwich a few days ago. This rare moth has previously been seen over these sweet-smelling white flowers; it loves to poise above them on whirring wings and push it long 'tongue' down the tube. This is a favourite method of sipping with the hawk moths; one of the smallest of them is called the hummingbird, for it hovers just like this tiny bird above the blossoms. Another has for its specific name *Sesqui pedalis*, (the Latin poet Horace's coining, meaning unusually lengthy) for its proboscis is 18 inches long; this, however, is not a British species.

Thomas Coward

A wonky wasp

ℰ◌ OCTOBER 1917 ◌℘

Someone had taken a wasps' nest in Kew Gardens. Perhaps as he carried it home some of the inmates objected, or he discovered that most of the cells were empty; at any rate it had been dropped and lay broken by the path. Over the grubless cakes a few weary workers, chilled by the night exposure, crawled feebly, and three young queens refused to leave the ruins of what had once been their home. They seemed puzzled by the tragedy that had overtaken the busy colony, but they were too weak or too stupid to fly in search of shelter. Two of them died quietly in my killing bottle, but it was not until I pinned the bodies on a setting board that I discovered that one was abnormal. Either through an accident in her youth or from birth, she was a cripple; the second and third legs on the right side were missing. Imperfectly developed insects are not rare; but the interesting point about this wasp was that she had made the best of a bad business. When she was alive, I did not notice anything peculiar about her gait, but when I attempted to set her limbs, I noticed that the third leg refused to remain on the left side. It was only then that I found that the right legs were missing, and that, in order to avoid the bias of three legs against one, the third left leg was bent under to work on the right side. I was sorry that I had not kept her alive to watch her manner of walking.

A Carnarvonshire correspondent writes that he saw a few swallows about a week ago, and having seen some remarks in the Diary about late swallows, sends me the note. It is not late for stragglers; we often have some passing in November, though of course the majority have departed. We can with fair accuracy say when the last swallows go, for they are day-flying migrants. It is not easy to tell when many other species leave us.

Thomas Coward

Lady Milkcart

ೞ October 1917 ಯ

The barometer was falling at the weekend, and yet on Saturday the sun and wind combined to make an ideal day for fruit-getting. Many worked, as we did, from early morning till dusk. Since then, storms of wind and rain have swept over the country. This morning we found that a large proportion of what fruit we had left was on the ground; yet still, owing no doubt to the heavy leafage remaining on the trees, there are both pears and apples that have weathered the storm.

I find, from very recent enquiries, that farmers in Cumberland and Westmorland have come through their labour difficulties exceedingly well, owing to the ready help given them by their friends and neighbours in all ranks of society. To see a lady of title drive a milk cart and at a pinch shoe her own horse, and young and old take

The squire's wife takes over from the milkman

their share of the work, rough or smooth, as they have done now for months past, shows that there is no degeneration in the race.

There are, this autumn, some who are finding it difficult to get horses for agricultural work, and also to get motors at the time they most require them. I would suggest the use of draught oxen where possible, for they are no difficulty to manage and will do good work.

Arthur Nicholson

Searchlight and moonbow

ဆာ OCTOBER 1917 ର

Beams from the searchlight stabbed the dark storm cloud in the west, when, last Thursday evening, a correspondent was walking homewards. While watching these, he noticed one faint and narrow beam that at first he attributed to a more distant searchlight, but, when he reached a darker portion of the road, where gas lamps no longer confused his vision, he saw that the beam had a distinct and regular curve, which, growing clearer, became a perfect arc. Looking behind him, he saw that the moon had just appeared above the housetops in the east; his beam was a lunar rainbow. When the weeping stormcloud reached him and, passing over, obscured the moon, his observations ended. He asks if the phenomenon is rare.

Possibly the necessary combination of falling rain and moonshine is not frequent, but there are other reasons why it is seldom noticed. Fewer observers are abroad in suitable places for noting lunar than solar rainbows; when rain falls in sunshine we look for the beautiful prismatic arc; at night we turn our collars up and trudge on to shelter. The rainbow, whether in rain, the spray of a waterfall or the breaking waves upon a rocky shore, attracts the attention of the most casual people; the faint beam at night only of those who look out for nature's phenomena and wish to understand them.

The same writer noticed one day recently that a large bird had dropped in the ditch-intersected meadow opposite his house, and on further investigation put up what, from his description, was undoubtedly a heron. This voracious hunter of frogs, rats, small fish, and beetles travels far in search of suitable hunting-grounds; I am not surprised to hear of it in this position of the Mersey valley. I often see it high overhead, apparently travelling in a leisurely manner, but really getting through the air, with deliberate but powerful wing-beats, at a great pace. On quiet Cheshire meres and marshes it is a common bird, but it also knows food-providing ponds and ditches everywhere.

Thomas Coward

CHAPTER FOUR

FIT FOR HEROES

In the scientific literature on pheasants, there is an interesting study from early 1919 of the effects of distant noise on a pen of the birds in Sussex, well inland from the coast. The reverberations that unsettled them came from the controlled destruction of captured German munitions at La Courtine, more than 60 miles away on the other side of the Channel. It was a fitting symbol of the end of the first world war and the devastation it had brought to so many lives and to the countryside. These effects were certainly not ended when the guns fell silent at last at 11am on November 11 1918, but there was no immediate social or technical revolution in rural Britain. The old order and its accompanying drowsiness had been given a long and vigorous shaking, but they proved resilient in the new land that the prime minister, David Lloyd George, had promised would be 'fit for heroes to live in'. Thousands of hectares converted to arable land during the submarine siege reverted to pasture and many small farms abandoned newfangled tractors in favour of the much-loved traditional horse.

The great drive to grow corn slackened immediately, as foreign imports once again became accessible and cheap. By 1934, home-grown wheat had reached its lowest price at market since records began in 1646. As part of the coalition government's attempts to forestall the spread of the 1930s slump, following the great crash on the United States stock exchange in 1929, marketing boards for the main crops were set up between 1931 and 1933, but English farm-ing remained in the doldrums for the rest of the decade. The pictur-esque landscape was much remarked-on by new visitors to the countryside – weekend tourists in the small saloon cars that were newly on the mass market, and parties of cyclists encouraged to explore by the socialist Clarion Club and similar groups of enthusi-asts. They found tea or a glass of milk at quaint farmhouses, almost always with a dark, dignified dining room with maple-framed engravings of Queen Victoria opening parliament or Highland cattle standing in a burn. They noted the piles of lumber and scrap equip-ment, which occupied the place that beaten-up cars with birds' nests in their radiators have on farms today.

If these tourists' routes took them over the Sussex downs, they would have found throughout the 1930s that the air was musical with sheep's bells, still used on flocks in the county until the second world war. Shearing time gave the opportunity to watch hand-clip-ping in many parts of the country, where small farmers preferred to hire temporary, skilled shearers instead of clubbing together to get expensive but sometimes unreliable machinery. The old methods gave visitors the chance to see different styles with histories as vener-able as the dialects and folk songs that academics were busy collect-ing from villages at the time. Kent alone had the Marsh Shear, used in Romney marsh farms, which started the cut at the animal's head, and the Uphill, more common further inland, which saw the clipping begin at the belly.

Oxen only stopped hauling ploughs in 1929, when a Major Harding pensioned off his team at East Dean farm, inland from Beachy Head. They were the last survivors of 12 oxploughs recorded in Sussex in 1912. Earl Bathurst retained his six Herefords for ploughing at Cirencester for a few years longer, but they were more of an aristocratic eccentricity and tourist attraction than a genuine help on the estate. The same could not be said of horses, whose fight against the tractor was one of the most dogged last stands of the 20th century. In the flatlands of Lincolnshire and Cambridgeshire, horses were still used in preference to lorries by a handful of commercial carters. On the farms, shires and smaller breeds pulled a fascinating variety of wagons, carts and wains. Perhaps the most extraordinary was the 'muffer' or 'mophrodite', terms derived from the Greek hermaphrodite meaning both male and female. This was a vehicle formed by joining together an old cart and haywain to make something that was neither but both.

Horse teams as large as 25 animals could be found hauling mole ploughs to make drains, and others stood patiently tolerant of the rich smell while farmers inland from Brighton used fishermen's unsold mackerel as top dressing for seed crops. They hauled equipment for ancient but continuing farming practices such as spuddling, a preliminary loosening of the soil for ploughing, and warping, the deliberate flooding of riverside meadows just before seeds were broadcast. Scything could still be watched, with the mesmerising rhythm achieved by veterans of the craft, and in Essex there was still a daily 'gleaning bell' rung at the village of Farnham until 1931. Gleaning was a traditional perk in low wage days, a free-for-all in the fields immediately after harvest when old methods left plenty of grain for scavenging. The bell rang at 8am to allow the gleaners into the fields and 6pm to warn them to leave. Pride and the setting of standard wages after 1917 by the first Agricultural Wages Board sounded its knell, except in isolated pockets, such as Farnham, where traditionalists stood out. Almost as rare by the 1930s was the 'horkey' or free harvest supper provided by farmers for everyone who had helped get the crops in. With regulated wages, most landowners reasoned, there was no longer any need for such generous gestures.

The colour of the countryside was also little changed, as most of the unusual crops introduced during the first world war to counter shortages did not long survive the coming of peace. Teazles, used for wool-combing on account of their finely hooked seedheads, had briefly become an extremely valuable crop because the traditional French teazle fields were converted to food production during the war. A bale of 20,000 teazle heads cost £20 by 1919, but had slumped to £5 within five years as continental production resumed. Flax, which had been encouraged in the flatlands round Selby in Yorkshire and on the Somerset levels during the war, also fell back. There was no longer emergency demand for aircraft and balloon fabric, hospital linen or extra linseed for oil and cattle food. The fields of soft blue flowers, which so resemble a lake when seen from a distance, retracted and farmers reacted in their customary way. 'The industry is in a bad way now for the same reason that has been fatal to the best traditions in British agriculture,' wrote one of the Yorkshire growers. 'The public demand is for cheap inferior foreign stuff, instead of more expensive but sound and lasting goods.' Catherine Harrison, a young veteran of the Women's National Land Service Corps, the first world war's land girls, remembered at the time how her team had worked all hours in the flax fields in 1918 '... feeling that the whole fate of England depended on us. A few months later, after the armistice, we had the mortification of seeing in every drapery shop window: For Sale. 100,000 yards pure flax aeroplane cloth – surplus government stock. Eight pence a yard. Perfect for durable underwear.'

At least there was no war any more. But the horrors of 1914-18 could not be forgotten, with many villages looking after shellshock victims, inconsolable widows and amputees, whose presence was for many years a reminder of the terrible events. Every community, too, was involved in the organisation of war memorials, from public playing fields to the gift to the National Trust of the entire mountain massif of Great Gable to honour the fallen. And in 1930 there was a recessional link to Britain's earliest recorded organised line of battle, when Boudicea's tribesmen painted themselves with blue woad before battle. The country's last commercial growers of the grand old herb closed in Boston, Lincolnshire, when their final contract for woad to dye policemen's uniforms expired.

We're not slacking in the north

ᎦᎤ JANUARY 1918 ᏣᏴ

For some days we have had softer weather with only a slight frost in the early morning, but the keen east wind has not added to the pleasure of outdoor work for the average gardener wanting to make a good start during the holidays. This morning there has been no rain, so we are trying to burn rubbish, a necessary work now greatly in arrear. In a recent speech, Mr Lloyd George expressed the opinion that we who were at home were having matters more easily as time went on, and wanted rousing to an effort greater than ever. This does not apply, at all events, to the north of England generally. Efforts here during the past nine months have been increasingly vigorous.

On Sunday I passed by a field of some six acres, which up to last spring had from time out of mind been a pasture. Then a farmer living a mile away took it, and got a record crop of potatoes off half of it last summer. Since December he has ploughed the lot. Known throughout the county for the excellence of his stock and his able management of his farming, he is a good example of what is being done by those who have land to cultivate – small patches or broad acres – from Crewe to Carlisle. The premier, I am sure, will find that as regards this part of the country tonnes more food will be produced in the coming season. Alongside our own ground is a field that up to last midsummer scarcely served for more than a pasture for horses. It has now been made into a chicken farm on modern lines with a population of plump birds.

Arthur Nicholson

Money for jam

✇ JANUARY 1918 ✇

The alternating spells of frost and sunshine have continued through-out the past few days. By sundown yesterday, we had the extra unwelcome presence of a heavy snowfall. It was preceded by a drop in the temperature and then followed by sleet and rain in great quantities. This has fortunately had the effect of washing the roads clean and this morning there were many places where I found signs of rainfall lying in pools on the half-thawed surface of the pastures.

It is well that the suggestion you read yesterday, made by the chairman of the Royal Commission on Sugar Supply, should be more widely known – that private fruit growers, who are now unlikely to have sugar allocated to their fruit and jam-making, should begin at once to get all the sugar possible out of their own cupboards and stores to use for this purpose, for after this week to retain it will be considered hoarding. In some places in this district, unfortunately, inspectors came during the fruit season last year and gave everyone positive instructions that no sugar kept back or saved from ordinary supplies was to be used in preserving apples and blackberries and the like or for the making of jelly from these fruits. In the case of crabapples to my certain knowledge, a very heavy weight of good fruit was wasted.

Arthur Nicholson

The spread of the owl

ᘒ FEBRUARY 1918 ᘕ

With February came the primrose, polyanthus, blue periwinkle, daisy and snowdrop, and the yellow jasmine is a mass of flowers. On these sunny, mild days we have felt the approach of spring. Nor has the song of many birds been wanting. We have been mowing rough grass off a field, no doubt exposing a supply of insect life and seed that these little friends are always on the lookout for. From morning to night, small parties of thrushes have been busy there, and every bird in the neighbourhood seems to have visited the field in some part of the day.

The gooseberry trees are showing small buds, and on all fruit trees there are clear indications of where we will have bloom later on. We are glad still to have frost during the early hours each morning – that will, we hope, keep back a dangerously early development. Those who have a few bits of land vacant may be reminded that a few gooseberry trees are quite worth putting in at this season, but the planting must be done at once and with care, spreading the small roots out so that they may not cross one another, and using some light earth and leaf mould that it may hold a fair supply of water should dry spells occur in the coming season.

There are in our district so few keepers in this wartime that our friends the owls are increasing in numbers, and as they have for the past 30 years been having a better time, I think we may now safely say that both the barn owl and the tawny owl are to be found everywhere – even in some cases breeding within the limits of quite large towns. As they are, of course, night feeders, sometimes they escape the notice even of those whose premises they occupy.

Arthur Nicholson

Seaweed medicine

☙ MARCH 2004 ❧

Nothing visible except the path at my feet and the seat that General and Madame De Gaulle used in 1969 during their Irish holiday in Cashel House Hotel. Here they sat, enchanted by the view – for me obliterated by a shining membrane of silver mist. Slowly it divided, layer after layer rising, it seemed, to join the rising sun. Then the glory was revealed – Cashel bay with its small islands, its Atlantic waters washing the enclosing shore, the light pale silver on the still sea, changing to a glittering hardness until the sun, at last fully risen, turned the surface to soft gold. What beauty, what gentle joy, what heart-nurturing peace.

Later we walked, noting the little fields, hard granite stones, rocks, and the high distant peaks of the Twelve Bens. In a clearing we saw a small, roofless stone cottage, history intruding to remind us that the simple dwelling was famine-emptied in the 19th century, when famine succeeded famine to culminate in the Great Famine of 1845-1852. What busy, hard lives the people of pre-famine and post-famine times led. Séamas Mac-an Iomaire, a native of Connemara, writing in the first quarter of the 20th century, in his book *The Shores of Connemara*, lists at least 33 kinds of seaweed. Its harvesting by hard physical labour was almost year-round. It was, of course, used as fertiliser and was also made into kelp, from which iodine was extracted. A tonne of kelp fetched £12 during the first world war. Mac-an Iomaire writes that at the end of April, 'If the sea is troubled as it comes ashore on an ebbing tide, you will see women, men and children out to their armpits in the mouth of the waves,' gathering mayweed.

Sarah Poyntz

Back from the front

෯ NOVEMBER 1918 ෬

The steady rise in the barometer we hope indicates a continuance of the fine weather, for though it is accompanied by a fall in the temperature, light frosts will aid the ploughman, and it is his great autumn work about which we are anxiously thinking. Though we have at last a cessation of hostilities, there is in all European countries such a shortage of food that we must make every possible endeavour to grow food in our own country. The success we have had in the past 12 months ought to be a great incentive. Although the weather during the past two months has held us back, we may expect to have more help in the coming time and be able to work and plant more ground than for many past seasons. Some of the first to return from service will be the young farmers, and many who have been working at munitions and other war work will be able to return to the land.

Arthur Nicholson

A happy ending

A recent visitor, a regular reader of this Diary, after a long chat about the distant past of our schooldays, suggested that I should write something about the impact of the first world war on our little town, or on the now practically extinct west Oxfordshire dialect. We got on to the subject of nicknames, once more commonly used than Christian names hereabouts, and one we remembered was Pusser, for Percy. This conjured up memories of Pusser, a member of the local platoon of the territorial army, marching with the squad to the station where a troop-train was picking up local units. I remembered that the leader of the party marching through the town also possessed a nickname – Glory Thornett – and, possibly in contravention of King's regulations, led the party with fixed bayonet to which the union jack was attached. Although the TA was formed for home defence, these volunteer reserves soon found themselves in the trenches on the western front. Pusser was illiterate, and borderline in intelligence, and when it came to writing home he had to dictate the censored letter to an officer. The latter was obviously familiar with the local speech, and transcribed Pusser's letter verbatim. It was to his mother, also illiterate, and she took it to the local newsagent and stationer, a general adviser to our community, to read to her. The shopkeeper had copied the letter and years later read to me the final portion of the letter. It read 'Dussent thee worry about I, our mam – I be all right – I keeps my yed well down.' Thanks to this precautionary behaviour, Pusser returned and I remember his wedding drive through the streets in a colourful Oxfordshire farm waggon. 'Yed' for head reminds me of another incident. Having moved house, we gave our goat to a neighbour, and once when passing his house I saw a little boy playing with Billy. It butted him from behind and sent him flying. He got up, rubbing the seat of his trousers, and exclaimed 'My God 'is yed's 'ard.'

Bill Campbell

Spinning out rations

ᔆᏇ DECEMBER 1918 Ꮗᔆ

The extensive use of 'kindle-wood' and other timber to make our fuel rations spin out may, as a side-issue, influence the number of insects and other invertebrates next season. Old and fallen branches and trunks with loose bark, especially when slightly rotten, are the winter refuges of an immense number of small animals; we not only destroy their shelters but also cremate the sleeping victims. Much of this latent life is in the egg stage, but many insects hibernate as larvae, pupae, and in their final, perfect state; beetles burrow into the wood itself or mine the timber beneath the bark; woodlice and spiders, centipedes and millipedes, slugs, and even worms hide in cracks and crannies. Some of these are our foes but many are our friends, and all alike perish in the flames.

When cutting up a block of oak, I came across a dense knot of earthworms, flaccid and lethargic; they had found a spot where the damp had entered and rotted the hard tissues. I turned them out and a robin came to investigate but did not seem to care too much about them; a blackbird or thrush would have provided decent interment for the lot. It seems a pity to destroy useful creatures such as spiders, worms and carnivorous beetles but, after all, what is useful and what harmful? The predacious animal does not care about economic values; it devours other carnivorous creatures as well as those we think are our enemies because they feed on plants. Some of our worst pests destroy weeds as well as edible vegetables. The ways of nature are apt to be complicated.

Thomas Coward

Dark winter

☙ DECEMBER 1918 ❧

I have heard people make disparaging remarks about the laurustinus. It is, to my thinking, one of the best and bravest of the dark season shrubs. It is evergreen but with shining, cheerful leaves. It flowers not at one particular moment but in a desultory way from October to Easter. This makes it, I admit, less romantic than the flower that one can associate more particularly with a loved season. But there is a steady consolation in the firm, robust, rather hard and bright cheer of its coral buds and snowy white blossoms. It suggests the fresh cheek and white linen and brisk courage of the best sort of hospital nurse. There is no sentimentality about the laurustinus but much steadfastness. It is there to smile at you and give you its confident support in a season of blizzards and mists and dismalness.

It has begun to flower early this dark and terrible winter, and one says grace for it as one does for all the brave encouragers.

Helena Swanwick

The greatest memorial

☙ OCTOBER 2006 ❧

The Fell and Rock Climbing Club of the English Lake District is 100 years old this year, its record for philanthropy and helping hill-lovers access Lakeland's mountains second to none. What dragons it has fought along the way – although it has not always been successful. The Styhead motor road was one such 'dragon breathing fire', according to the *FRCC Journal* – in 1919 the committee passed several resolutions to help destroy it. Yet the controversial road from Borrowdale to Wasdale was given the go-ahead.

Great Gable – the biggest war memorial in Britain

Work had already started with the widening of the road at Seathwaite when war broke out in 1939. According to the late Stanley Edmondson of Seathwaite farm, 'Only Hitler saved the day.' How that Styhead road, had it been built, would have been congested – and especially next month. It is in November when walkers and climbers throng the summit of Great Gable for a non-denominational service of remembrance.

The war memorial first came up in the FRCC committee at New Year 1919, when attention was turned to honouring those who had fallen. Various ideas were discussed, emotions ran high and letters were written to the *Manchester Guardian*. Then an intriguing avenue presented itself: to purchase a block of high fells that, once acquired, the FRCC would transfer to the safe keeping of the

National Trust. In October 1923, the documents of title were handed over to the trust – covering more than 3,000 acres (1,200 hectares) of open fell above 1,500ft (450m). The ceremony was held at Coniston, where the club was founded in 1906; the first informal meeting was held at the Sun Inn.

Tony Greenbank

Traces of tragedy

ॐ DECEMBER 1999 ॐ

The massive carnage of the first world war continues to raise echoes wherever you travel in rural France. We had stopped by the church in Scrignac, a small, Breton stone-built village close to the centre of the peninsula. Having a brief interval before our 4 o'clock rendezvous, I got out of the car to stretch my legs. The church dominates its hinterland in the usual style. The village war memorial faced me, and I started to read the names of the fallen engraved on the stone pillar (almost 200).

I noted the dreadful recurrence of war casualties for some families. The engraved names showed that the Auffret family recorded the deaths of five young men through the years 1914-18. There were other local family names that also occurred more than once but not with the scale of sad repetition with which the alphabetical roll commenced.

Despite ongoing rural depopulation, there are Auffrets in this year's phone book still living in the scattered farming community of Scrignac. But what scarring of traumatic grief that family must have carried through the early decades of the century, which also saw such postwar imbalance that a generation of young women had reduced chances of finding a husband.

There are few French rural villages that do not have a war memorial to match the one I was reflecting on in Scrignac. The charnel house at Verdun was only one of the killing fields that accounted for the death of so many of that generation.

My father, born in 1898, survived the last two years of war on the western front and I remember that all through my school days Remembrance Sunday always saw him weeping in the garden shed for the pals he had left behind in the Flanders mud.

'Some bastard should have hung for it,' he used to observe, and he was not thinking about the enemy of the period but reflecting rather the theme of lions led by donkeys in Alan Clark's *The Donkeys*.

Colin Luckhurst

A lost world

ஐ JUNE 1998 இ

Across the cattle-grid, along the track, across empty pastureland and past the substantial, four-square farmhouse, I sat in a dark cider-barn (still functional) and heard how the owner had lived on this farm for 61 years. His grandfather, a carter, died young of pneumonia, and the widow was given a shilling a week by the parish. His father blacked boots at the rectory one day a week in return for breakfast, left school at 13 to work on the land, and often enjoyed a trussed and cooked blackbird for his packed lunch. In time, he went to the war, and afterwards demonstrated his acquired countryman's skills and instinct for good husbandry sufficiently to be granted the tenancy of a small county council holding under a scheme for ex-servicemen. In 1937, now with a young family – including Bertie, my informant – he heard that a larger, privately owned farm nearby was to let. He cycled to Castle Cary and impressed the agent as a sound man to recommend to the owner, who offered a fair deal. So the family stepped up to Higher Farm, 60 hectares, 35 cows, and a steady living to be made by their cooperative effort with one horse to do the mowing, harrowing and carting and provide family transport on occasion. She would trot at a steady 13mph to Castle Cary. One, or sometimes two, men were employed. The only paperwork involved chequebook and paying-in book and the only representative of officialdom was the local policeman. Everything was done by hand – milking, pulling weeds, making hay, building sheaves and roofing ricks. The second world war brought men with maps to decree that certain fields of choice pasture be ploughed for wheat. This was more than the horse could do. The ministry supplied an iron-wheeled tractor. Mechanisation, intensification, specialisation, quotas and regulation followed. Now there are no cows and the pasture is let for 'grasskeep' at falling prices.

John Vallins

All quiet on the western front

ஐ May 1938 ൙

The Somme battlefield still wears an air of desolation. But those whose interest lay in natural history found great consolation here during the war, in pursuit of their hobby whenever time and opponents allowed. Those woods that remained standing used to be full of birds, and nightingales often showed the bold side of their character by replying in song to any outburst of machine gun fire. Here and there lie rusty shell cases, and on the tin roof of an ancient and insecure dugout a blackbird was sitting on five eggs. For a long period in the war this fine wood at Havrincourt escaped destruction, although that part through which the front line passed was felled. Golden orioles were not uncommon and their fluty whistle still rings through the wood. Common, too, were nightingales, garden warblers and chiffchaffs; cuckoos called all day, and green woodpeckers gave their loud laugh, a cry that was greeted on one hazardous occasion with the caustic comment: 'Aye, you can ... well laugh.' Today, all these are there and two lovely golden orioles were the first birds to greet us as we drew near to the wood. A pheasant crowed among the trees and another in Logeast wood, a few miles away, a bird that, so far as my experience went, deserted the woods around the trenches in wartime. Wood pigeons flew out from the edge of the wood, though there are now no gullible and enthusiastic subalterns to report them as enemy carrier pigeons to Brigade Intelligence; the study of ornithology should obviously have its place in the Sandhurst curriculum.

Arnold Boyd

CHAPTER FIVE

STANDING ALONE

Memories of the slaughter in the first world war were so intense in Britain throughout the 1920s and 1930s, when masons had only just finished cutting the rolls of honour on the thousands of village memorials, that there was a deep reluctance to believe that the nation might have to confront a resurgent Germany again. If there was an element of sleepwalking into the first conflict, the prelude to the second world war saw more of a deliberate reluctance to wake up. This was especially true in the countryside, where the partial return of traditional ways after the great upheaval in 1914-18 had come as such a great relief. But there were also men in the villages who had served in the trenches and who, although marked by the horror of their experiences, knew that history gave little credibility to the notion of a 'war to end wars'. If all else failed, they were ready to take up arms again.

One of them was Thomas Coward's successor as the Country Diary's chief recorder of Cheshire, and especially its bird life: Major Arnold Boyd, a big, military-looking man, who got down to writing on the subject of Hitler with a sense of resignation and a good joke. If only the posturing dictator had been a bird man, too, he pondered wistfully in the column that registered the start of the second world war in September 1939, then he might have delayed things at least until the end of the autumn migratory season, which was so interesting to decent Germans and Brits alike. Boyd's unruffled humour survived for all the hard seven years of the global conflict, almost twice as long as the first world war and, for the English countryside, far more radical in its effects. He quipped in 1941 that the flight to Scotland by the Nazi party's offical leader, Rudolf Hess, might have been influenced by bird migration (nicknaming him in passing the 'Party Leaver'). It is a sense of humour shared by one of his fellow wartime diarists, Gwen McBryde, a merry widow in the farming business, who careered around on her caterpillar tractor and enjoyed finding resemblances to Nazi leaders in peeling potatoes. Her husband, who died very young, was the best friend of MR James, the provost of Eton and King's College, Cambridge, better known for his ghost stories. Some of these are set in the countryside round Gwen's farm at Dippersmoor Manor near Kilpeck, in Herefordshire's Golden Valley, which is now a delightful B and B.

These two were central to the column's close reporting of the war's effect on rural England, which was much more detailed in the second world war than in the first. Although there was fighting every day and much suffering, it seldom reached the relentless pitch of the slaughter in the trenches, which everyone on all sides had watched aghast but been unable to halt. After the initial scares of invasion, the drama of the blitz and the performance of the RAF 'Few' in the Battle of Britain, a conviction set in that victory was a matter of time and endurance. The *Guardian*'s high command did not share their 1914-18 predecessors' feeling that readers wanted a 'war-free' zone in the Country Diary where they could linger among birds and flowers. The second world war was also far more of a 'people's conflict' and vignettes of what was really happening to evacuees and Italian prisoners of war in the countryside were appreciated, and revealing. The team was strengthened by John Adams, a teacher and later *Country Life* writer, who suffered from ill health but initially sent his entries from Fighter Command bases, where he was stationed until invalided out in 1943. George Muller, a naturalised German who was reckoned the best fly-fisherman in the north of England, combined his Country Diary entries with fire-watching on his beat in Cumbria. Ronald Garnett, a retired Manchester textile manufacturer, did the same in Yorkshire's North Riding, where he also helped with the Home Guard. Like Boyd, he refused to allow the Nazis to spoil his natural history hobby, reflecting shortly before D-Day how, unruffled by the war, 'the itch to go searching for an early wheatear recurs each year.'

The landscape they described in the early years of the war was one under attack. The whole of the south coast was an armed camp and parts of it suffered regular bombardment from big guns on the other side of the Pas de Calais. Dover alone had 3,053 warnings of shelling during the war. Villagers were on the lookout for parachutists and spies and were enlisted to help make triple defensive lines of pillboxes, which are still landmarks in today's countryside, concrete and usually disappointingly smelly. Their lives were regulated by one of the great success stories of wartime bureaucracy, the 'WarAgs' or county War Agricultural Committees. One of these was appointed for every county, with a brief to decentralise as much of its power as possible straight away. More than 500 district committees thus emerged, with four to seven members who all lived locally.

Each of them then took responsibility for monitoring up to 50 farms, mostly small, so that the average amount of land overseen by an individual was 2,000 hectares. The effect on British agriculture was galvanising.

There was always a danger of abuse, given the committee's draconian powers – which included requisitioning entire farms – and the countryside's tradition of local feuds. But the government incorporated an appeals system and engaged as a watchdog the rural press, which was curbed in so many other fields of reporting: for example, descriptions of enemy action and bomb damage were bafflingly vague. The WarAgs involved local people in discussions of the best crops to grow and the most suitable places to grow them; they organised the large temporary labour forces of land girls and prisoners of war, and they endlessly offered advice. For an industry steeped in tradition, it was a tonic to have real agriculturalists arrive at every farm – the WarAgs visited them all – and offer an audit of best practice and fresh ideas for improving methods and yield.

The helping hand was sometimes bitten. By 1943, requisitions meant that WarAgs were directly running some 160,000 hectares, although this was a relatively small proportion in the context of the government's aim – successfully achieved – of getting 800,000 new hectares under plough by April 1940. The target was achieved in spite of bitter weather in January and February that turned the ground to stone. Farmers ploughed after dark with shielded lamps and special permission from air raid precautions to work on moonlit nights. Very rarely, the requirements of the WarAgs were blocked altogether. One tragedy, after prolonged attempts to negotiate, was the shooting dead by troops of a Hampshire farmer called Walden, who was besieged after he refused to accede to the local committee's demand that he plough up one and a half hectares of meadow to grow crops.

A separate issue in the early years of the war, in a landscape shaped to a surprising extent in many places by hunting, was the question: will the hounds still be able to go out? The problem was not so much one of disrupting food production, as of the war's toll of killed or captured hunt officials. Among them was the Duke of Northumberland, who was master of the Percy hunt in the north-east, and the Earl of Coventry, who mastered his family's pack, the Croome, as well as the Hawkstone otter hounds in the summer when fox-hunting was off-season. Among suggested remedies was the idea of a 'flying pack' of hounds that could stand in for local hunts whose officials were absent. It came from Countess Maud Fitzwilliam of Wentworth Woodhouse, near Rotherham, who even suggested a name for them: The Spitfires.

If only

⁊ SEPTEMBER 1939 ⳡ

I cannot help thinking that if only Hitler had been an ornithologist, he would have put off the war until the autumn bird migration was over. I wonder if any of the friendly Germans whom we met last year at the International Ornithological Congress at Rouen feel as I do. That he should force us to waste the last week of August and the first fortnight of September in a uniform that we hoped we had discarded for good is really the final outrage. This morning I stopped for five minutes on a causeway between two pools and there I saw a ruff and snipe in scores and had the luck to spot a garganey flying with a spring of teal; just an inkling of what we are missing elsewhere in our favourite haunts.

A correspondent living in Didsbury has had quite the unusual fortune of seeing a Camberwell Beauty (*Nymphalis antiopa*) flying into his garden. This butterfly is a real rarity, which occasionally comes to England as a migrant from the continent (where my correspondent has seen numbers of them), but nowadays there is always a suspicion that an English-caught one may have been bred in England from imported pupae and released. There are about 20 recorded instances of its appearance in Lancashire and Cheshire, but so far as I know, no recent ones. There was evidently a notable immigration in 1872 but since then the records are few.

Arnold Boyd

Farewell to the swallows

ℰ❍ SEPTEMBER 1939 ℭ℞

The lights are going out all over Europe, but they are being relit in many a garden and olive grove all along the northern fringe of the African continent, for the small songsters that have graced our countryside during the summer months will now be well on their way to their winter quarters in the south. No doubt most of them will be silent, or at most will make use of those soft notes known to birdwatchers as sub-song. The earlier broods of swallows and house martins have gone; for some days they could be seen in numbers on the wires or skimming along the surface of the village beck, but now only a few late-breeding birds sweep up to nests beneath the eaves or into the cow-sheds or pigsties on the farms. There has been war even in our small garden, for the robins, in freshly moulted plumage, have been staking out their claims to winter territories. There have been intermittent bursts of song, much 'ticking' among the trees, and posturing of birds with head and tail cocked up in an attitude of aggression. No doubt, too, there have been protests made to those seen flying over neutral territory. One bird, which carries a metal ring is, I think, a bird of the year, for most of the older ones carry a coloured ring as well, indicating that they have visited the trap on more than one occasion. So far none of these has yet appeared.

Ronald Garnett

Pantomime helmet

℘ NOVEMBER 1939 ℘

Out of the north has come has come the earliest smew that I have ever known. Rarely do we see smews in Cheshire before Christmas, and often a week or two of January has passed before one of these ducks appears on a Cheshire mere. It was on November 5 that I saw a low-swimming bird, in appearance somewhat like a grebe, as I was passing along the road at the end of a large mill dam. My glasses at once showed me what it was, and also that it was the youngest smew that I have ever seen. It cannot have been hatched before June or July, as its plumage showed, for it lacked the black patch behind the eye that is such a feature of the adult duck or young drake; the feathers of its crown were short, and had not acquired the bright chestnut colour that will come later, and its face was not really white.

The Soul-cakers' play on All Souls' Day almost died out during the first German war, but was kept alive by a band of stalwarts in the village of Comberbach. This war finds a troop of youngsters in the same village equally determined to keep the flag of the Soul-cakers flying and to maintain unbroken the annual performance of this ancient rite. New faces have appeared beneath the Old Woman's bonnet and behind the greasepaint of the Black Prince, who wears a German helmet captured more than 20 years ago. The Wild Horse still indulges in his strange capers as the band passes from farm to farm and from local hall to the village inn.

Arnold Boyd

A refugee from the Nazis

ഌ DECEMBER 1939 ൫

Just after Munich, a black-headed gull was picked up beside one of the meres bearing a ring that showed that it had been marked in Czechoslovakia. As I recorded in these notes at the time, it came from part of that unfortunate country known as 'Zone 5', but after the German occupation full data of the bird were at last obtained. Now another gull has been found within 10 miles of the place where last year's bird was discovered: on its ring, which was issued from the museum in Prague, were the letters CSR (Czecho-Slovakian Republic), showing that even the birds of that country still carry evidence of their birthright. We shall probably have to wait till the end of the war before full details of date and locality of ringing become available. Ornithologists should be allowed to disregard man-made frontiers like the birds themselves, or at least to have a clearing house for information at Geneva or The Hague.

Arnold Boyd

The gull traced

ഌ FEBRUARY 1940 ൫

A stranger walking along the Cheshire hedgerows might reasonably wonder if we kept a race of giant rabbits in our meadows. When the snow was at its worst three or four weeks ago, they had access to no grass at all and lived on a meagre diet of bark, and now the bushes are rabbit-bitten five feet from the ground, where the hungry animals had climbed the snowdrifts in their search for food. They have damaged the newly laid hollies in the hedges, and already have killed young apple trees. No wonder that some of the farmers set 'grins' (wire nooses) for them, but these are wicked traps and may just as easily catch a dog by the foot; sometimes even a cow's tongue is caught in the cruel noose and almost cut in two.

A report has been received of the ringed Czechoslovakian black-headed gull that was found at Northwich at the end of December; it had been marked at Bohandec, some 35 miles due east of Prague, in June 1936. Another ring, found on a starling in mid-December last year, has just been sent to me. It was from Rossiten, the famous ornithological station in East Prussia, whence so many ringed birds have reached England in the past.

Arnold Boyd

Saving our bacon

ᏽᎦ March 1940 ᏽᎦ

The news that bacon was to be rationed was widely broadcast and evidently reached the ears of Sally, our four-year-old sow. A week ago she farrowed and produced a family of 19, her best score to date, although she has never failed to bring up a big litter. The local farrier (as the Cheshire farmer, often a Liberal in politics but a thorough Conservative in language, still calls the vet) maintains that 10 are enough for any sow to rear, but Sally has before now reared as many as 14 at a time. Now, however, we have had to call in outside aid and deprive her of some of her children, which in her patriotic zeal she has provided to excess. The evacuees are having a grand time at a neighbouring farm, where they live in front of the kitchen fire; they have quickly taken to cow's milk and have learned to sit up for their bottle.

These hand-reared piglets become astonishingly tame. We gave special food to the rit of one brood (the little one known in other places as the runt or reckling, and by other names) and it very soon knew its name. As soon as a voice called 'Roger, Roger' over the loose-box door, there was a heaving in the heap of youngsters sleeping in a pile in the corner, an anxious eye appeared, and then Roger shook himself free from his brothers and sisters and made straight for the door and the special dish he knew was waiting for him. None of the others moved at all. If you get to know them, pigs can be most engaging and friendly animals.

Arnold Boyd

Ploughing every patch
ဆ MARCH 1940 ର

The dalesmen are coming to the end of their ploughing of land that has not carried crops since the end of the last war. Under the precipitous face of a mountain where peregrine, buzzard and raven breed, is turned over a strip of ground that would seem to be almost uncultivable. It is so stony as to suggest that at some time it was the bed of a mountain stream in roaring spate. 'Aye, it is taking a lot of doing,' the flockmaster told me, 'but the neighbours say that in 1917 and 1918 it paid for the labour put into it. And I ken a place verra like it which a fella of newfangled ways cleared and nothing would grow on it. Nature's queer. It was as if stones had come there on purpose to help seed to sprout and corn and taties and turnips flourish amain.'

'You can have too much of a good thing,' he went on. 'I mind last war having a grand crop of oats in a field that had not been ploughed since the days when Irish folk came over at harvest to work for twopence-halfpenny a day. It was too grand. There was a terrible storm of wind and rain, and three quarters of the crop was wasted. I divvent think that beans sown with the oats to steady them would have saved that crop.'

George Muller

Exciting new veg

കൊ MARCH 1940 ౭

The humble and prolific Jerusalem artichoke is much in the news these days. Like a film star, it has its worshippers and detractors. By those who like its flavour it is said to rival the potato in nutritive value and to produce half the crop with half the labour.

There are three kinds of artichoke grown in this country for culinary purposes. The Jerusalem artichoke (*Helianthus tuberosus*) is a member of the sunflower family and its tubers are proving an invaluable standby just now when vegetables are so difficult to obtain. Its tubers are left in the ground during the winter and dug as required. The Chinese artichoke (*Stachys tuberifera*) is a member of the mint family, and its small roots are lifted as required, as they do not keep well in store.

The globe artichoke differs altogether from the other two and in growth resembles a giant thistle with very large greyish leaves and stout stems, which bear large terminal, fleshy flowerheads, which are the part used as a vegetable. Seeds sown in early April outdoors will not produce flowerheads in the first year, and a quicker way to obtain a harvest is to increase the stock now by planting the tubers in a prepared bed three feet apart each way.

MA

The partridges' war

കൊ MARCH 1940 ౭

The golden retriever, a few yards ahead of us in a snug spinney, stopped suddenly, put his head to the ground, and then lifted and brought a screaming creature to his master. The prize was a quarter-grown leveret covered with saliva. 'Good fellow', exclaimed the gamekeeper. 'The tenderest-mouthed I have ever had'. The leveret was set free on the ground, and although he could not have been much more than a month old, he legged it hard over the plough, sticking, as far as the naked eye could judge, to one furrow all the way to the top of the heave of land. The gamekeeper pointed to the plough. 'The only good thing about the war', he said. 'There will be more food and cover for the partridges, and if we have anything like a favourable summer, there should be some grand broods. All this grazing land in peacetime is no good for partridges. Farmers round up their livestock in fields and the young partridges get trampled over. The worst is that vermin will thrive amain as they did in the last war. Stoats and weasels are wick enough as it is. They take a lot of keeping down and I shall have to let my traps stay put all year through. I killed 32 last week.'

PS The first of the early host of sand martins arrived on the 20th of March.

George Muller

Farmers' market

April 1940

At the end of the last war certain counties were becoming very active over the problem of distributing and marketing surplus eggs produced in cottage gardens and on large estates. It does indeed seem tragic that we cannot pick up the threads from these ventures, here and now, and get some workable schemes in motion. In the country districts of the south it is a burning question. Those who already grow as much as their household can consume are ready and anxious to produce an infinitely greater quantity but see no organised way of disposing of the surplus. Sporadic efforts to start a local stall, as has been done so successfully by the Women's Institutes, will undoubtedly arise. But it needs much more than this.

We need to be told in precise terms what we ought to grow, and we need vigorous guidance from an authoritative source as to how each county could and should organise cooperative buying and selling. We need instruction on how the surplus can be graded and sent to a local stall at a market or sold wholesale to the tradespeople. Above all we want to be urged to get such machinery in motion at once.

Many people would be delighted to produce more for the good of the country, and many unemployed and older men would be delighted to turn an honest penny by cultivating unused ground and selling the result of their labour. Lack of guidance on these two matters will cancel out much of the enthusiasm generated by the 'Dig for Victory' campaign.

MA

The fire watchers' cats

ഇ MAY 1940 ൝

Mop, Sop, Tottie, Winkle and Tiny are the tortoiseshell cats that keep the fire watchers' mill free of rats. When, 18 years ago, the present tenants came, the place was full of vermin. Seed potatoes stored in an upper room disappeared in a night. The sound of the rolling of tubers across the floor to holes in the walls suggested burglars were afoot. The team of tortoiseshells, consisting of the grand-dams and dams of the company of today, changed all that. Within a few weeks, all the rats were gone. Yet even now, hordes of pink-soled rats are to be seen of a summer's evening slipping along a damp, mossy trod at the foot of rock plunging precipitously to the river, on the way to another mill stuffed full of all that is to their liking. They have a broad water between them and their enemies. But rats that know no better swim downstream to the mill. Once they are marked to ground, their day is over. Mop is the captain of her side. She sits at the mouth of a hole waiting with inexhaustible patience for the moment when her victim must emerge for food and drink. Her spring never misses. Today she brought five rats at intervals to the lawn. Give me cats before terriers. The tykes are all right at stack-thrashing time, but they are clumsy on other occasions. And a team of cats needs so little upkeep. A saucer of milk a day, and for the rest, rats, mice and the lampers, eels and trout of a shallow mill lade.

George Muller

Escaping the war

ꝏ MAY 1940 ꝯ

I spent last weekend looking for long-eared owls in west Lancashire. Careful search of several small fir spinneys failed to produce any, and it was only after much hesitation that I decided to go and look at just one more spinney, a small but dense one about a mile away. As soon as I entered it, I knew that there was an owl of some sort about, for the ground below not one or two but about half a dozen trees was littered with pellets. I began tapping the tree, and soon an owl flew out of one of them and made off to the far end of the wood. I followed it and, picking on a tall tree with a dense top as the most likely for it to have flown to, looked up into it. And there, sitting close against the trunk, its eyes blazing fury, its 'ears' erect like some devil's horns, was my long-eared owl at last. For some time it stood stock still, gazing at me; then, disturbed by some slight movement of mine, it flopped down and flew silently to another part of the wood.

In the neighbourhood of these spinneys, I came across five birds I had failed to find along the Ribble valley. Corn buntings 'jingle-jangled' from field posts, reed buntings spluttered from posts beside streams, yellow buntings wheezed from hedgetops, whitethroats rattled from the depth of hedges and a solitary sedge warbler chattered from a bush at the side of a stream. Here I saw also four wheatears, which I am satisfied were the Greenland form, and three whimbrel. The whimbrel flew over me, heading north and calling as they went. There has probably been a big passage of them just recently, for I hear flocks of up to 20 were to be seen on tidal flats in Cornwall and Devon a fortnight ago.

John Adams

Better times for hedgehogs

෨ JUNE 1940 ෬

There is no doubt that the slower one moves about the countryside, the more one sees of its detail. Just two years ago when motoring north to Scotland my companion and I were much struck, as we neared the border, by the number of hedgehogs that lay crushed upon the road. We supposed that they had become bewildered by the headlamps of motors that passed that way in the darkness. Last week I had ocular evidence that this was not necessarily the case. Returning homewards on a bicycle from our market town just before dusk, I came upon a hedgehog doddering along in the middle of the tarmac road. I got off and stood watching its behaviour for some time, shielding it from the passing traffic. When a car and even an enormous bus passed by, causing a great draught of air, it stood quite still with nose lowered to the ground ready to curl up at a moment's notice. Obviously this procedure was likely to cause its certain death, for each time it remained long enough for another car to arrive, and cars are not as numerous on the road as they were two years ago. Before leaving, I dropped it into the hedge bottom, hoping it might take another course when it at last ventured to unroll.

On another day I found two downy pheasant chicks upon the road, but they had their own protector. The hen came flying out of some long grass and ran around me showing much agitation while I lifted them into a field over a wall. If she had other chicks concealed, which no doubt she had, she would see that the party was safely reunited in due course.

Ronald Garnett

An interesting billet

ஐ June 1940 ൦

To be stationed in a busy town such as Birkenhead is not an ideal existence for one whose chief pleasures lie in the country. Houses and docks are not the surroundings a bird-lover would choose, but the most unlikely places provide birds with food and nesting places – the two essential attractions. There is a wide stretch of ground by Seacombe ferry on which nothing has yet been built and where weeds and the alien plants found in many seaports grow profusely. I had never before thought of the yellow wagtail as an urban bird, but here there are at least half a dozen pairs, and today I watched one of them carrying food and another pair walking about in a cobbled street – an incongruous sight.

Meadow pipits are breeding there too, and yesterday I picked up a fledged youngster from among the long grass, and there is one pair of skylarks to 'startle the dull night' and enliven the sentries just before dawn. I have watched a pied wagtail carry food to a nest in a big coal stack, but the only other birds that are based in this part of town are house sparrows and starlings; an old starling accompanied by two of its family ambled along in a croft and repeatedly popped a titbit into the mouth of one of its followers, and today a sparrow was feeding one of its babies on a housetop.

Arnold Boyd

Colour in the docks

ഇ June 1940 ൬

There is a flower garden even in dockland. One corner of a waste-land over which I occasionally have to walk is completely covered with plants of melilot – at the least an acre of yellow flowers. Their profuse growth is a marvel. The plants grow so thickly that it is necessary to push one's way through them; in height they must aver-age five feet and some are between six and seven feet high. Among these are a good many plants of the alien white melilot. The two are much alike except for the colour of the flowers, but I found that the trefoil leaves growing out from the stems of the white-flowered plants were slightly the longer and narrower, and in no case did these plants attain the great height of the yellow-coloured ones. Clover and trefoils flourish on this deserted plot; clover, both red and white, and the yellow bird's-foot trefoil everywhere. Toadflax, so often a plant of the roadside waste, is plentiful; not so showy as our garden snapdragons. But a charming flower all the same. There are occa-sional plants of the dyer's mignonette, and the rosebay willowherb has been fully out for a week, though not so abundant on this partic-ular piece of waste as might be expected. It seems to flourish best among cinders or on fire-devastated land.

I have watched a yellow wagtail carry food under a big coltsfoot leaf and at last found its nest – incredibly well-hidden in the lush herbage, which had grown greatly since the nest was built; unless the bird had shown the way, no human eye could have detected it.

Arnold Boyd

Murder on the river

ဆၢ July 1940 ⓒ

To lie at ease in a punt and be gently propelled down a lovely river by the slow dexterity of a skilled punter is surely one of the simple delights of this life. Our placid enjoyment was rudely shaken when we glided past a knot of little boys throwing stones at a brood of moorhen chicks, with evident intent to kill. A unanimous shout of protest caused them to scurry under the willow trees. A moment after, we passed a group of elderly gentlemen fishing from the bank. This charming scene seemed to add to our pleasure and we passed by murmuring our approval. Why did we condemn one sport and applaud the other? Both called for skill, quickness of eye and hand; killing was certainly the object of both groups. Destroying the chicks was perhaps more blatant murder, but to angle for trout was only murder surrounded by a certain guile and deliberate fraud. The well-fed gentlemen were not in need of food – that was all too obvious; and quite possibly the children would have preferred to handle a split cane rod if their pocket money could have run to such a luxury. No, I think we were ill-advised to condemn one sport and laud the other.

MA

Rallying round

ဆာ JULY 1940 ର

As the summer crops in private gardens mature, the problem of how to dispose of the fresh vegetables and fruit not needed by the householder is proving a difficult one to solve in some districts.

A village in the south of England has taken matters into its own hands and is organising the collection and disposal with great success. A committee was formed of producers and a voluntary secretary appointed. The secretary produced a rough census and timetable of produce likely to be available for marketing. She was fortunate in having some reserve sources, such as large gardens not usually wishing to market, and some professional market gardeners from whom to make her contacts. She established a collecting, grading and packing point in the village and received the surplus produce there twice a week. She soon found that the best outlets for the produce were the semi-wholesale consumers such as hospitals, schools, Army depots and the Naafi. All these were able to arrange their own transport and she, by her careful census of the produce available, was able to supply specified amounts each week.

The gardener's job these days is not only to produce food but to arrange to get it to the consumer as cheaply and in as good condition as possible. This can only be done through cooperative effort, and these isolated ventures should be linked with legally recognised county organisations.

MA

Playing soldiers

ৰু August 1940 নে

Every few days there is some fresh flower to see by the Birkenhead docks. A big clump of tansy of most luxuriant growth, many chicory plants, and one plant of the greater knapweed, a rare plant in Cheshire and much more beautiful than the 'hard heads' (the common knapweed of our meadows), have all come into flower recently, but the little broom known as the dyer's greenwood, for long a feature of one bank, is now well past its best. A tall plant with yellow vetch-like flowers was quite new to me and was identified by an expert, to whom I sent a cutting, as the sickle medick (*Medicago falcata*), another rarity in these parts.

Near the coast in a narrow ditch, the pink sea millwort was flowering profusely, the blue sea aster had come into flower, and nearby the round-leafed mint was growing – a far from common plant, with soft and rather wrinkled leaves. The plantains that grow so freely in such a place were of four distinct species; the most plentiful was the sea plantain (*Plantago maritima*), with long, narrow leaves, and with it grew the buckshorn (*P. coronopus*), with a rosette of divided leaves; and there were plants of the greater plantain (*P. major*) with big broad rounded leaves and of the common ribwort (*P. lanceolata*) with whose flowerheads I used to play 'soldiers' (a variety of 'conkers') as a very small boy.

Arnold Boyd

Bull's eye bombing

ಜ AUGUST 1940 ಚಿ

Two bombs that fell on a field in a rural district harmed nothing but the crops, but local indignation at this proof of Boche unscrupulousness was unbounded: 'Eh! Just fancy! Bang in the middle of Ford's clover root. These Jerries will stick at nothing.' The farmer is in no doubt about the value of what he grows, but he does not care for a bomb's help in digging for victory.

Another thing that greatly impressed the neighbourhood was that the two bombs 'fell in a dead straight line' on the ground; though how two of anything could fail to do that is hardly clear.

Arnold Boyd

Handing out the fruit

ಜ SEPTEMBER 1940 ಚಿ

On every side one hears of excellent schemes for making the fullest use of surplus vegetables and fruit grown on allotments and in private gardens. A practical experiment has been launched in Monmouthshire for distributing this good food among dependants of men now serving in the forces. The local horticultural society and the allotments association volunteered to give any surplus they might have and plans were made for a lorry to tour the allotments between the hours of six and eight every Wednesday. The surplus is deposited in distributing centres in the poorer districts of the borough. Each week the Citizens' Advice Bureau supplies a list of 50 persons likely to benefit from such gifts, and cards of invitation are issued to attend at the distributing centres according to the quantity of produce available. The Salvation Army sees to the distribution.

When there is any surplus after these distributions have been made, it is sent to the local military hospital. This family distribution scheme has been in operation three weeks and supplies of vegetables have been given to 110 persons.

From Cambridgeshire I hear that vegetables are collected for dispatch to the crews of submarines and minesweepers on the east coast. Similar schemes to these are developing all over the country to the great benefit of all.

MA

The air-raid warden's dragon

❧ SEPTEMBER 1940 ❧

It is surprising how ignorant are some of the country folk in regard to common objects of the field and woodland. An air-raid warden comes each night to sleep at the post where hangs the large dragonfly of which I wrote last week. One or two had no idea what it was, while others asked if it would attack a man. Several knew the local name of 'horse-stinger', which I did not. Nor can I exempt myself from the same charge of ignorance, for last week I was brought in a sprig of oak on which was a cluster of three galls in the axil of the terminal leaves. Oak apples are, of course, familiar, but these appeared somewhat like fir cones, and turned out to be artichoke galls, caused by the fly *Andricus fecundator*, which attacks the buds. I am told that these galls are commonly seen in Surrey, and perhaps it is only my own blindness that made me think I had made a discovery. One of the wardens, who works in the forestry, tells me that he has often watched the fearsome-looking pine sawfly laying her eggs. Having inserted her long ovipositor in the bark, she spins round in a circle so rapidly that she becomes a blur, and sawdust is ejected from the hole. He added that her egg-laying tool is left in the hole, but unless all her eggs are laid together, this is scarcely credible. From a police constable I heard the story of how a nest of house martins that had been broken and the eggs scattered was quickly repaired by the efforts of no fewer than five birds working together. It sounds like a story of the people of London at the present time, whose heroism is the admiration of us all.

Ronald Garnett

Pozzie and burgoo

ಒ OCTOBER 1940 ೧೪

Although the army in the first German war made some use of rhyming slang, it was not allowed to displace many of the old soldiers' words derived from service in India. Some of them, it is true, are still current; in the battalion in which I am now serving, porridge is always 'burgoo' and jam is 'pozzie', but instead of 'rooty and muckin' for bread and butter we hear of 'Uncle Ned' or 'strike me dead' and 'roll-in-the-gutter'. The rot had begun 25 years ago. Tea was then almost always known as 'char', but even so I can well remember a sergeant's saying he had got some 'Tom Thumb in his i-diddle-dee' when he had scrounged some rum and put it in his tea. But 'looping-the-loop' for soup must be a new phrase; it is certainly prevalent today. 'I want some squad halt in my looping-the-loop,' is the modern way of asking for salt in your soup.

Utter inconsequence has always marked this form of slang. There is no reason why 'pig's ear', any more than any other rhyme, should mean beer, but it has long been as well-known as 'apples and pears' for stairs. These latest additions, however, are more lunatic than ever.

It seems strange that 'roll-in-the-gutter' should be in such demand that it has earned a place on our ration cards.

Arnold Boyd

A mighty store of jam

ဆာ OCTOBER 1940 ရာ

It has, of course, been a wonderful year for plums, and our Women's Institute has by communal effort converted the fruit into more than 3,000lb of stoneless jam. No wonder then that the blackthorn branches are laden with grape-blue sloes, the more conspicuous since the fall of the leaf. The rowan trees, too, have been laden but birds of several species are rapidly stripping the berries. It was among these that I saw the first autumn redwings on October 2, 10 days

Stirring for victory — the WI and their jam

earlier than I found them last year in the very same trees. Here too, only yesterday, I found a brambling among some chaffinches and with them, a party of bullfinches and two more redwings. I sat down on a stump to watch and presently a pied woodpecker with crimson nape took up his stance on the rowan tree bole, leaning far backwards on his tail to preen the feathers of his breast between bouts of digging into the bark in search of insect food. Some jays came into a neighbouring oak seeking the acorns, but it did not take them long to spot me sitting there, and they were off. Both swallows and house martins have remained into October and the latter still show interest in the nests beneath the eaves, though only, I fancy, as a possible place for a night's lodgings.

Ronald Garnett

Nature study in the bomb crater

🎗 NOVEMBER 1940 🎗

We have just been examining the curious effects resulting from the explosion of a number of small bombs that fell in a woodland copse. The small symmetrical crater was ringed round by the now familiar mound of earth and the surrounding bracken and grass was mown close to the soil. About 30 yards away from the crater, a large number of beech saplings had had their heads cut cleanly off with a cut that ran parallel to the earth and not, as one would have supposed, at an angle to it. The larger trees that had the misfortune to find themselves in the path of the shell splinters received deep, clean cuts often six inches deep and the width of the bole.

Already the damaged trees have received first-aid treatment at the hands of their owner. With a sharp chisel and hammer, he cut away all the jagged edges and smoothed over the cavity with a pruning knife. The largest holes he filled with cement to keep out the rain and painted the exposed parts with Stockholm tar. With the coming of spring the bark will gradually heal over the ugly scars and the trees should be none the worse for their adventure.

MA

An evacuee's view

So NOVEMBER 1940 CR

A youth evacuated to the Yorkshire moors from Surrey writes to tell of his impressions:

'One begins to realise after frequent moves from one place to another,' he says, 'that all town is monotonous and boring and that every strip of country has its collection of vital interests. The speed with which the mountain becks of Yorkshire rise after even what may appear to be quite a temperate fall of rain must be seen to be believed. I have watched the stream transform itself in two hours from a broad-bedded meanderer, splashing gently between the rocks, into a full, rushing torrent that would do credit to many of our smaller rivers.

'On a day such as this, when the mountains and fells are brought 10 miles nearer by a liberal dose of heatless winter sunlight, one's time is by no means wasted in going up on the moor and collecting a bundle of dead heather. It is easily picked, breaking cleanly at the root. It makes a preferable substitute for paper when fire-lighting, giving a hot, fierce flame. Occupied in this pleasant task, I disturbed frequent flights of snipe, flying off in their peculiar corkscrew motion. Grouse, too, flapped heavily away from me giving a weird cackling laugh. Had I been a stranger walking on the moor at night, I might have thought it was some evil spirit leering from the darkness.

'I came across a rabbit standing upright by his burrow, thumping the earth with his hind legs. This warned other rabbits, which may not have observed my cautious approach, that danger was at hand. I have known tame rabbits strike the bottom of their cage when a bomb burst nearby, in an instinctive effort to warn their fellow-creatures of impending danger.'

MA

Ploughing the park

⨯ DECEMBER 1940 ⨯

The parkland slopes gently to an occupation lane. It is free of timber. When the country house was built centuries ago, the master had an eye to an uninterrupted view across the river. Hares were crossing the fine pasture to the plough beyond. Rooks dug and pigeons searched for food. A blue haze drifted from a fire of crackling thorns. The dressers of the hedges had partially completed their work. The layering of the branches is left for spring. The tenant of the home farm looked wistfully on the scene.

'We have to plough out the park for the first time in living memory. The War Agricultural Committee wants another 7,000 acres on top of the county's 28,000 acres this year. This park is full of "management" – so full that they reckon it will grow two white crops without fertiliser. No doubt about that, but shan't we miss watching the Irish cattle waxing fat? Man, how beasts and sheep did come on once they settled down on this pasture! You could hardly believe your eyes. They have put on flesh amain. And now we shall have nobbut a sea of oats. Well, that's war, and we shall have to eat less meat and more porridge.'

George Muller

123

CHAPTER SIX

THE LONG HAUL

The peace of the British countryside in 1941 was frequently interrupted by a long drawn-out whistle, followed by a splintering crash. It was a sure sign that the Local Defence Volunteers were out practising with their simple but murderous weapon, the Northover Projector. Issued only to the LDV, better known as the Home Guard or 'Dad's Army', these were essentially sawn-off drainpipes solid enough to take a small explosive charge, which fired anything from a grenade (the officially intended ammunition, but initially in very short supply) to cricket balls, or, on at least one occasion, a bust of Shakespeare's smoothly rounded bald head. The whistling became a national feature after a Post Office unit of the LDV discovered that milk bottles made excellent practice missiles, complete with the realistic sound effect of an incoming artillery shell as air swirled round the open mouth of the flying bottle. Rolled-up newspapers were also used, less dangerously and in the larky spirit of Captain Mainwaring's fictional TV unit. Magistrates had to deal with at least two cases of Northover newspaper missiles knocking off village police constables' helmets.

The Home Guard was usually regarded fondly by communities that had a traditional suspicion of most forms of authority, largely because the units were made up of familiar faces. With the exception of young men serving in the regular forces, an LDV detachment would often be the village cricket team in khaki. Its members seldom bridled at the nickname for their initials, 'Look, Duck and Vanish', and were well-attuned to the countryside and their particular local landscape. Many spent hours in exercises of a Boy Scout or Romany traveller variety, digging pits concealed by brushwood or devising tripwires for parachutists whose effectiveness was fortunately never tested. Lord Dunsany, the celebrated writer of fantasy fiction who was an enthusiastic member of Dad's Army, wrote an anthem for rural battalions of the force that drew on their beautiful surroundings and suggested a uniform in keeping with these. 'Give us for badge what some child's hand might gather in our fields,' he started, adding:

Give us no star of blazonry
Of Crown or crest, but let it be
Rather some simple blend
Of Traveller's Joy and bryony,
Or such wild blooms as feed the bee
On hills that we defend.

The amateur manoeuvres of Dunsany and his colleagues were part of a wider and increasingly professional defence network in the countryside, much of it covert. Unknown to passersby, engineers

126

from the General Post Office climbing up telephone poles to maintain lines were actually cutting selected ones off. Subscribers affected were told only that their connection had been 'reserved for the War Department', with compensation but no appeal. The commandeered lines proved their worth during the Battle of Britain and again in 1944 when rapid communication about incoming V-1 flying bombs was essential for the crescent of barrage balloons and anti-aircraft guns defending London. More humbly, they served key local personnel such as Grace Hatley, the schoolteacher at Wood Ditton, east Cambridgeshire, who became the village's chief air-raid warden and thus held on to her line, Stechworth 4, for the duration.

The adjusted telephone poles were part of a vast operation shown to a party of journalists, including the *Manchester Guardian* war correspondent, Evelyn Montague, in the 'Spitfire summer' of 1940. He described 'a strange new countryside, a countryside stripped and armed for defence against the invader'. Camouflaged trucks and jeeps stood in orchards, road blocks guarded the approach to villages, a battery of howitzers was dug in under leaf and bracken-strewn netting with the guns targeted on a nearby bridge, ready to destroy it should Nazis land and approach the river crossing. The scale of the defences was far larger than any passerby would have imagined. Montague wrote: 'Driving along the country roads between fields of corn, one wondered where the soldiers were.' It was not until his party had been briefed by a senior officer in an innocent-looking country house that was actually regimental headquarters, that they realised that 'men were manning trenches and strongpoints hidden all over the countryside.'

Montague concluded that the architects of Britain's homeland security, as it would now be called, 'had taken all the possible forms of invasion into account', but others were not so sanguine. In the countryside surrounding Bradford, the local branch of the

Independent Labour Party was tipped off about shoddy workmanship in local air-raid shelters carried out by unscrupulous contractors who had skimped on both time and materials. The city council dismissed the allegations as defeatist talk, so the ILP commissioned engineers from Bradford Technical College to carry out a survey. They found that 28 shelters had been made using unsuitably soft bricks, four had loose bricks, 46 had soft mortar and 13 had serious structural problems. Continuing bluster by the authorities subsided when the Professor JBS Haldane visited the city and was photographed by the Bradford Telegraph & Argus crushing an air-raid shelter brick in the palm of his hand.

While the need for defences added many new features to the country landscape, it removed others. Road signs disappeared for the duration and an even more notable absentee was the sound of church bells. Within weeks of the declaration of war, the bells were silenced so that they could be used as a modern version of the ancient beacon system in the event of invasion. Prominent clergy, including the Archbishop of York, protested but to no avail. Exceptions were allowed only to celebrate the victory of General Bernard Montgomery and the Eighth Army at El Alamein in November 1942, and on Christmas Day the same year. But by April 1943 members of parliament were under pressure from their constituents to win more concessions as the prospect of Nazi parachutists or Panzer tanks storming ashore grew ever more remote. Churchill himself sympathised, telling the House of Commons: 'I cannot help feeling that news of anything serious such as an invasion would leak out.' So restrictions were eased but it was not until Victory in Europe Day, on May 8 1945, that full peals were finally allowed at any time.

The ban extended to the traditional chiming of the hour, which left the nights in isolated villages very quiet for volunteer fire watchers, who included two of the *Guardian*'s Country Diarists, George Muller and Ronald Garnett. They and others put the long hours to use by noting the timing and number of nocturnal bird calls, surveying owl movements and putting the world to rights. Garnett managed a little astronomy too, in spite of wartime distractions. He described how, 'In these days when so many things are flying about into the night sky, a meteor is likely to go unrecognised.' In country towns, night watch duty could become quite convivial; a telephonist from Middlesex, HJ Brown, recalled for a history of the Post Office how his local exchange was manned overnight by a duty maintenance engineer, two or three fire watchers and three Home Guards. He remembered: 'We developed our own way of passing the time – some were card fiends, some were Monopoly addicts, some delighted in fry-ups of any sausages etc they could get – and some just liked to argue.'

A final feature of the countryside during the long haul as the imminent Nazi threat was faced, receded and then finally turned to preparations for the allies' own invasion of occupied Europe, was concealed for different reasons. Contraband was everywhere, including probably some of the sausages fried up by Mr Brown's overnight watch party. Each household was allowed to keep one pig but required a licence that docked a number of meat coupons issued as part of the national food rationing system in March 1940. Recollections compiled by Age Concern in rural Shropshire tell a story of illegal second or third pigs kept in secret sties, flitches of pork hidden in babies' cots, malicious informants and sudden calls by inspectors from the Ministry of Food. One farmer near Shrewsbury was notorious for black-market pork until his cache was found hidden down the farm well. Poaching also flourished with the reduction in numbers of gamekeepers. Village diets were supplemented with pheasant, rabbit and hare in preference to

Spam, the tinned meat imported from the United States and distributed with eloquent testimonials and recipes from Lord Woolton, the vigorous Minister of Food. These failed to prevent the bland concoction's name becoming a synonym for ghastly food and a joke that lasts to this day.

Bash a rat

❧ JANUARY 1941 ❧

Our War Agricultural Committee appeals to keepers to spare stoats and weasels to help the campaign against rats. As the preservation of game has been an uphill business since the last war, it is likely that the committee's suggestion will be approved. A keeper finds it difficult to keep his hands off vermin, but with so many mouths to feed he will do all he can to put rats out of the way, and he will at least refrain from setting his traps in the hedgerows. It is difficult to estimate what havoc stoats and weasels do among rats. One very experienced and skilful gamekeeper reckons that a stoat or weasel is not less successful among rats than is a peregrine on a moor, and the hawk, he says, kills a grouse a day.

But for the wholesale destruction of rats we have to depend not a little on the effectiveness of the measures taken when stacks are being threatened. The wire netting put round a stack the other day was accountable for a result far better than it was imagined could be forthcoming. For all their sense the rats would not leave until the last forkfuls were being lifted. Underneath was a horde doomed to perish.

George Muller

Tobruk, Tobruk

℘ JANUARY 1941 ℘

We have recently acquired a refugee. Some local gunner with more ammunition than sense had succeeded in winging an adult common gull, and the poor bird was found wandering helpless in one of the village gardens. We patched it up as best we could, cutting off the damaged flight feathers of the damaged wing to prevent them from trailing on the ground, but I fear it will never fly again. It has settled down in a way that is really surprising, and as it seems to be omnivorous we have found no difficulty in keeping it supplied with food. A dead long-tailed fieldmouse was swallowed head first, and a small piece of chocolate pudding from the 'hen bucket' seemed to be much appreciated. Rabbits being in good demand, it is an easy matter to obtain a paunch or two, and we hope the gull will become a permanent ornament to the garden. Gulls caught young are useful in a garden, for they do not scratch like hens and are light enough on their feet to avoid trampling the plants. I remember two herring gulls that lived in the yard of a cotton mill on the Ribble, which snapped up the unsuspecting sparrows that came to steal their food. Guinea fowl are noisy birds and their call is often as persistent as a corncrake's, but I was amused to hear one, as I passed a farm, calling 'Tobruk, Tobruk, Tobruk'; a bird of ill omen to Italy, perhaps.

Ronald Garnett

A happy evacuee

℘ JANUARY 1941 ℘

I have been up to the New House with a small offering to Mrs Maplethorpe; it is her birthday and she is 60. She left me in the big kitchen a moment, and returned with a jug of pinkish liquid and a small tumbler. She said I must drink some of the mead she had brewed, and insisted on filling a beer bottle with it for me to take home. You may not know what fermented and rather decaying honeycomb smells like, but mead tastes like that. She says she gives it to her lads in hot water when they come in wet and cold. At New House there is always something to be had for all comers. The post-man, after his tramp across the fields, breakfasts there, and the small evacuee boy from Merry Hungry who comes with his jug for milk goes off eating a cake or apple.

I prepared to depart, but first I had to go to the parlour to inspect some artificial flowers and a new bead lampshade. The room had a coal fire but was cold and gloomy. We crossed the beeswaxed oilcloth on a track of sacking, laid there to prevent marks being made by muddy boots.

The lampshade was discovered after a time. It was acting as a repository for bits of bills and jottings of fowls sold to customers. I walked home down the lane between the snowdrifts. The indefatiga-ble young of Merry Hungry had planted their footprints in the largest and snowiest drifts, but there were no wheel tracks in the lane and I picked my way back in the footprints I had made in coming.

Gwen McBryde

Confounding the paratroops

℘ JUNE 2002 ℘

From the neat summit-shelter on Scout Scar (230m), the limestone escarpment west of Kendal, a remarkable panorama can be seen: scores of Lakeland and Yorkshire peaks crowd the horizon, all round the compass. Every time I visit the scar in reasonable weather, I count the hills – from Black Combe to the Scafells, Gable and the Langdales, most of the eastern fells, the Whinfell ridge, the Howgills, Gragareth, the highest mountain in Lancashire, with the flat summit of Ingleborough, the Yorkshire giant, just peeping over the top, and then the Kent estuary and the open sea. Anybody who knows the hills pretty well should be able to identify at least 70 of them.

Ninety years ago, deciding, rightly, that this was the finest viewpoint in the district, local worthies built the elegant domed shelter that we call the Mushroom on top of the Scar to mark the coronation of King George V. It was vandalised recently, but the other day the restored memorial was unveiled to commemorate the golden jubilee of his granddaughter. The outline of the hills, now etched on stainless steel to deter a later generation of vandals, has been most accurately drawn on the 360°-view indicator. At least 120 hills are shown, as well as other features visible from the top, including Arnside viaduct and Blackpool Tower.

They say that during the second world war, the mountain panorama was painted over to foil German parachutists. I can't confirm this, as I was on the other side of the world at the time, helping out against the Japanese.

A Harry Griffin

Entertaining the troops

℘ FEBRUARY 1941 ℃

I have been removing the festoons of holly and the big bunches of mistletoe that were hung on the oak panels in my hall. The room is given up to soldiers who drop in from their Oxfordshire camp during the evenings. They write letters, listen to the news, go to sleep to the loudest blare that can be got from the gramophone, and drink tea and cocoa. We make a roaring fire of branches in the big open grate.

Lately, I have greatly enjoyed a game of backgammon with a Greek. Occasionally we have a sergeant and some bombardiers. All the boys are excellent company. But I am wandering from my subject of mistletoe. Formerly, it was never brought in until New Year's Day, and then the old bough, which had been allowed to hang in the house for 12 months, was taken out and burned. I always see that mistletoe is burned, as there is a theory that when eaten by cows it causes illness. It is said that all evergreen must be taken out and burnt before Candlemas Day, the second of February. I could not bear with them as long as that. I like to bring in Christmas roses and the branches of wintersweet and the honeysuckle, whose flowers so resemble the wintersweet, though they are borne on bare branches but are tucked away amongst the evergreen leaves.

BA

Drugs in the meadow

℘ MARCH 1941 ℘

I have been looking carefully in the lower meadow to see if there is any sign of the colchicum (meadow saffron) pushing up its strong green leaves. The plant is poisonous to cattle. For many years this land has been useless for early grazing and was put up for hay year after year. This colchicum, or autumn crocus, is charming when the leaves have died down and slender white-stemmed crocus flowers shine out of a mist in early September, but I decided that it must be got rid of. I was assured by the best authorities that there was no known means of doing this except by ploughing and picking out the bulbs.

In the last war, colchicum was needed for a drug, and a great many bulbs were dug up, with the strange result of causing the colchicum to flourish more than ever. There is no sign of them now in my meadow. I went round the year before last, pulling them and dropping a pinch of sodium chlorate into the socket, or simply dribbling a little of the sodium on to each plant. I expected to see a certain amount of seedlings come up, but there are none.

The team of white horses is jangling the roller over the meadow. It is one of the many pleasant sounds to be heard today. Plover are circling round, a robin sings from a thorn bush, and a ewe is calling her lambs.

Gwen McBryde

A good war for redstarts

&ℭ APRIL 2001 ℭ&

To some it would have looked like a dull grey bird, but to me it was an occasion for excitement – the first new species in the garden for two years. It was a black redstart, which perched momentarily on the roof then sallied off to reveal the flash of orange from which it takes its name. (*Steort* was an Old English word for tail.) It is a bird of rocky mountainous country, although like several species favouring this habitat – house martin and swift are two more – black redstarts have been able to exploit stone-made buildings as an alternative. Some of the first pairs ever to breed in Britain took up residence on the derelict site of the 1925 Wembley Exhibition. The population remained in single figures for about a decade until the Nazi bombers struck and the bird enjoyed a really good war. Black redstarts found the derelict buildings in the blitzed areas of London precisely to their taste and by the end of the 1940s there were as many as 30 singing males. They are famous for their odd nesting sites and have built on Dungeness power station, Aylesbury sewage works, the Palace of Westminster, Coventry Cathedral and Margate Pier. Another bizarre location was an old squashed bucket dumped on a new housing estate among the breeze blocks of a storm drain two metres underground. But my personal favourite is the pair that made a nest in the Millennium Dome area in 1999. Being a protected species, it almost threatened to delay building works and one suspects there are many, both in and out of government, who now rather wish they had.

Mark Cocker

The appeal of uniform

   🔊 APRIL 1941 CR

'And we know, Mr Weller – we, who are men of the world – that a good uniform must work its way with women, sooner or later.' So said the gentleman in blue, and what he said still holds good, but to 'women' must be added 'dog and cat', of either sex. There must be something subtly attractive about the rompers and forage cap of modern battledress, for no animal can resist them; no billet or cook-house lacks its bevy of hangers-on. Bruno, a terrier whose owner was taken prisoner in France, instinctively attached himself to the nearest men in khaki and soon picked out a new master, whom he never left and always warned when visiting rounds approached his sentry post, acted as his escort at company orders, and with his master was at last transferred to another unit. Then there was Narvik, a prolific tabby cat from a Norwegian ship, all of whose kittens were bespoke before birth.

A devastating air raid brought the homeless in by platoons. An attractive mongrel (a fox bull terrier) walked in that night and was taken at once on the strength for rations and discipline. He answers to the name of Blitz and is a friend to all the world. He and Buchanan, a black and white kitten, sleep side by side and eat from one dish, and he was sadly affronted when one cat rejected his addresses with a masterly right hook to the nose. The sirens alone make him bark. We also have Nellie, a little yellow bitch with a smug expression, and Nellie Wallace, another mongrel – so called to distinguish her from yellow Nellie rather than from any likeness to that admirable comedienne. All these animals, and I have mentioned only a few, scorn civilians. For them khaki is the only wear and their trust is never misplaced.

Arnold Boyd

Hens and the land girls

℘ MAY 1941 ℭ

A farmer's wife to whom I had given a bunch of daffodils once said to me: 'They say you get a duckling hatched for every daffodil you bring into the house.' It evidently was a prewar idea. I have only ventured on having one sitting of runner duck eggs, in spite of the fact that they are producing more eggs than the hens, but they are great wanderers and unpopular with the land girls when it comes to shutting-up time. The alteration to summer time finds them going down the meadow in procession to take a dip in the pond.

The big black hen to whom the task of hatching the ducklings was allotted sat out the 28 days with amazing patience, and has even thrown in two extra days in the hope that more ducklings would come out of the imprisoning shells. Her efforts were in vain. I had removed the four, lively, eel-like, little green ducklings that hatched first for a day and a night, but she has them now. They are hearty feeders and so far the hen is much gratified.

Gwen McBryde

Woman power saved the day in both world wars

Bombsite blackbird

On May 12 I visited the rocks at the river mouth at high tide. Since I was last there, many terns had arrived. A flock of fully 100 flew over the sea in search of a resting place and settled on a prominent rock not far from the shore. Most of them were common terns, and I could see only three sandwich terns, but I noticed what I am fairly confident was a roseate tern, though at too great a distance to let me record as a certainty a bird that has very rarely been seen in Cheshire. Two of the common terns went through a form of display; they stood side by side with their bills pointing vertically in the air – one of them with wings half spread – and there was a lot of chatter. A cormorant, in a flock of about 80, also did some strange posturing on a rock, with its great mouth opened wide to the sky. Today, in the same place, lesser terns were also diving.

On May 7, so a Wilmslow correspondent tells me, two cock pied flycatchers arrived there; it is always an event to see one in Cheshire, so he must have found it difficult to forgive the cat that killed one of them.

I am watching a blackbird's nest with interest. It has been built in a lamp, half of the glass of which has been broken by what is pleasantly known as enemy action. There the hen sits all day, completely indifferent to passersby.

Arnold Boyd

Massacre of the goats

My route took me past fields bordering the river Nairn, where the dippers, one of the earliest breeding birds in the Highlands, are now displaying. This could indicate they are now back in territory but in fact they stay in their territories most of the year. Bad weather, such as when it freezes, will drive them to the coast, but with the recent milder winters it has not happened for years. The fields on the banks of the river were devoid of birds, as if awaiting the influx of curlews, oystercatchers and lapwings. Brin Cliff towered above me at one point and I thought of the tribe of goats that once lived there. They were shot out in the second world war by officers billeted in the big house nearby – a mounted billy's head with huge, curved horns still adorns the wall above a fireplace.

Loch Ruthven looked bleak and inhospitable, with white tops on the waves, and it was good to reach the boathouse and the comparative shelter of the birch trees. For some reason I became ill at ease, but put it down to the fact that my senses were not working as it was too windy, and the waves were crashing noisily on the shore. A group of mallard rose from a sheltered bay, so close that they startled me. I could see the tails of the drakes, from which they get the local name of 'curly tails'. My feeling of unease strengthened and, as the hide came into sight, I viewed it almost with foreboding. For some reason, the dark, low building looked uninviting and I opened the door slowly as if I was expecting someone to be there – it was empty. The elements, rain and wind, were very dramatic but I could not concentrate: I felt I could feel a presence around me in the hide. I was glad to get back in the car.

Ray Collier

Wrecking a billet

ဆ AUGUST 2000 ဆ

You can count on the Women's Institute to lay on an invigorating trip. Last week we visited Chillingham Castle to see the wonderful restoration of this Borders pile, which has been in possession of the Grey family since the 1900s. As a child, I remember seeing its crumbling turrets spiking the racing sky as we piled out of the ancient Morris Minor and gaped enthralled at this marvellous, hoary, tottering building, the spirit of Border forays oozing from its very moss.

I went along with the WI to see the restoration undertaken by Sir Humphry Wakefield over the past 20 years. When restoration started, the castle was virtually roofless, with almost a tonne of pigeon droppings on each floor. During the second world war, soldiers were billeted here and were so cold that they stripped panelling off the walls to keep the fires burning. 'After extensive rot had been removed, 16 roofs had to be replaced,' Sir Humphry told me. 'But underneath the rotted Victorian and Georgian plasterwork we found medieval splendour. Great open fireplaces, passages and windows and one walled-up Tudor chimney containing over 100 documents and the oldest writ in Northumberland, dating from 1540.'

From one of the turreted stairways in the south wall of the castle I looked out of a casement window on to the beautifully restored Italian garden with lawns, clipped hedges of box and yew and the longest herbaceous border in the north of England. In medieval days, the garden had been a 'tilt yard' and on a platform at the west end wall, ladies sat to watch their knights jousting. Now there are rose beds and neat hedges.

Sir Humphry admits that restoration of the castle had been a Herculean task and, at the start, the resident ghosts had been hostile. 'They didn't like being disturbed,' he confided. 'But once I became constructive, they realised the ambience was positive and came on to my side.' Scenes from the film Elizabeth were filmed at Chillingham and when the cast were working in full costume, extra figures of that era were noticed in the crowd scenes. 'They were our ghosts mingling,' explained Sir Humphry.

Veronica Heath

141

A migrating Nazi
ᐯᐱ JULY 1941 ᐯᐱ

Till last Saturday I had not seen a clouded yellow butterfly in Cheshire since 1911, when I caught one at Parkgate in Wirral. One came flying across my home meadow, and later in the day I saw two more in the south of the county, both of which (as is their habit) settled on clover flowers and let me examine them at close quarters. In the same valley I saw a painted lady for the first time this year. Both of these butterflies are immigrants from abroad, and, exceptionally, arrive in large numbers. There is still time for this year to become a 'clouded yellow year' like 1877, when remarkable numbers visited many parts of Great Britain. We may expect the same thing to happen this year, now that they have the shining example of Party Leader (or Party Leaver) Hess to guide them to our shores.

Arnold Boyd

A rare outing
ᐯᐱ AUGUST 1941 ᐯᐱ

In these days of transport difficulties, it is seldom that a party of naturalists is able to meet together for fieldwork, and it was therefore a pleasure yesterday to join with other enthusiasts in a walk across country. One member of the party, no longer young, had overcome the travel difficulty by cycling some 80 miles the day before from the other end of the county, seemed as fresh as ever at the end of the walk, and was quite prepared for another ride of almost equal length the following day. Our leader, being a botanist, was able to show us some interesting plants, an especial rarity for the district being a small colony of *Polypodium calcareum*, a near relative, or perhaps a variety, of the oak fern. Among a number of flowering plants of the giant campanula we noticed that the finest head was supported by last year's dead spike forming a natural stake.

In a quaking bog of limited size were plants of both round and long-leaved sundews and a flower or two of grass of Parnassus, while nearby, among other species of orchis, were seen several flowers of marsh helleborine, some of which were already setting seed.

Ronald Garnett

Evacuees' treat

∞ AUGUST 1941 ∞

On a river trip near Oxford, two small evacuee children were especially delighted by weeping willows. They produced theories to explain the branching. They wished for Christmas when I told them that there was a Glastonbury thorn nearby, which is said to flower at Christmas. I was sorry that I could not tell them that I had seen it myself, but as second-best I was able to say that a friend of mine had seen some of the original Glastonbury thorns in flower.

When we stopped for tea, there was great excitement because a vole swam out from the bank some distance upstream, and we watched quietly while it swam nearer and finally completely encircled our punt. The children looked carefully to see just how it did its strokes and how it managed to keep its nostrils, eyes and ears just above the waterline. A guelder-rose bush was in the full glory of its polished, cherry-coloured clusters of berries, with some of its pretty, bright-green leaves near the berries becoming tinted with red. This bush attracted admiration and now a terracotta jug holding three branches of it graces our table.

BA

Nuts to the Nazis

❧ AUGUST 1941 ☙

These days one seems to spend an undue amount of thought on edibles. I take no interest in getting sandy cakes or chocolate that seems to require a helping of sugar, but products of the earth, usually so scorned by cooks, are interesting. Some, such as earthnuts, I learned to shun in the last war. I was sent out with a distinguished guest to show off the view. When we were about a thousand feet up, we stopped to rest, and I borrowed his penknife to dig for earthnuts. It was fragile and had long been used for cutting the pages of books. The blade snapped off before I had unearthed enough small, grubby rootnuts to cover the palm of my hand. My enterprising nursery governess served them on a saucer; shrivelled, greasy little morsels.

The recommendation to collect acorns and horse chestnuts caused a worse accident. There was a large, fatted pig ready to kill; her sty was under a spreading chestnut tree. Into her trough we emptied acorns, which she ate greedily, and we added some horse chestnuts to those already fallen into her sty. In the morning the pig was dead. Inflammation caused by acute indigestion, said the vet.

Gwen McBryde

Potato-head Goebbels

❧ OCTOBER 1941 ☙

The potato crop is so large this season that we have had to enlist any sort of help that we could get. Small evacuee girls with their attendant, smaller brothers came. Some of the girls bustle round and fill their pails and help each other empty the potatoes into sacks. When interest flagged, I organised races in teams for prizes.

There is one local boy of eight who is very serious-minded. He arrives on the scene and distributes empty sacks at intervals down the rows. He takes a proprietary interest in the place, and remarked to my bailiff that he thought one field was being planted too shallow, the seed not deep enough. There is a boy of five, Desmond. I had to invent mud forts and soldiers for him, and when I took him and some of the small children in to tea, he flung himself into a chair and said: 'I am completely worn out.'

The odd shapes of some potatoes lent themselves with slight additions to the representation of various things. We had a hippopotamus, a barrage balloon, mice and rabbits. There was a moose's head and a Dr Goebbels, and one fine V for Victory.

Gwen McBryde

To plough or not to plough?

❧ NOVEMBER 1941 ❧

The 'ploughing-up campaign' continues. Some farmers here still resent orders to plough certain of their fields. Often this is based on sound knowledge of the soil; a compromise is achieved between the farmer and the local War Agricultural Committee. Thus, in a number of pastures, boundaries are changing, because part of the soil is medium or light, well-drained and can be ploughed, while other parts are left under pasture because they give good pasture but have clay almost to the surface and are too badly drained for arable land. The meadow soil is then fenced off, usually by a fence of wooden stakes and a few strands of wire.

On one farm this has occurred in several fields. The stakes of some of the fences were split logs of larch, but in other fields they were substantial young limbs of willow. These had been removed recently, during pollarding, from the willows on the river banks. The willows were well thrust down into the clay subsoil. Many of them are now sprouting heartily, so that the uninteresting wood and wire fence is becoming a more attractive row of willows.

BA

Lord Haw-Haw

ཀ DECEMBER 1941 ཀ

For the past two days we have been able to study the behaviour, and also the appetite, of a hawfinch at very close quarters. A party of shooters, beating a wood for pheasants, came across a bird of this species that was unable to fly, though neither of its wings is broken. One of the party put it in his pocket and later brought it to me in a paper bag. Now in a cage, it seems entirely at home, and though I am all against the caging of wild birds it would obviously be foolish to turn it loose until it has recovered its powers of flight. It might indeed have been hand-reared, by its behaviour, for it does not dash itself about or even flutter when I put my hand into the cage to change the supply of water. Haws from a whitethorn hedge are its first choice of food, but rosehips are accepted as a substitute, and it comes readily to take either from my fingers. Only the kernels of the seeds are swallowed, the pulp and shells being quickly discarded, the nut of the haw being neatly split with a couple of sharp cracks. It was of course inevitable that the bird should be christened Lord Haw-Haw.

Ronald Garnett

CHAPTER SEVEN

DIGGING FOR VICTORY

Before he became prime minister on May 10 1940 after the collapse of Neville Chamberlain's government, Winston Churchill eased the frustrations of what he called the 'twilight war' by devising a series of extraordinary schemes and weapons that he thought might help to change the gloomy tide of events. One of them was a gigantic machine with the secret codename of White Rabbit No. 6, which was designed to dig a huge trench, 1.5m deep and 2.25m feet wide, to allow infantry and even tanks to creep up to the Germans' defensive Siegfried line without the machine-gun massacres of the first world war.

A prototype was approved by the government in February 1940 after secret tests of a scale model in a basement of the Admiralty in London that had been filled with sand. Weighing 100 tonnes and stretching 24m in length, the first White Rabbit, by now renamed

Cultivator No 6, ground along at half-a-mile an hour, moving 8,000 tonnes of soil in the process. Always an enthusiast for spectacular ideas, Churchill revelled in the scale of his new brainchild and was delighted to be given Cabinet approval for 199 more machines as a war priority by March 1941. There was a hitch, however, when the original plan to use Merlin aircraft engines to power the beast was derailed by the Air Ministry, which needed every available one for the Royal Air Force. But an even more powerful land motor was developed and the 'mammoth mole', as Churchill called it, was ready for the off.

Geological tests were carried out on the soil of northern France and Belgium and more than 350 companies were subcontracted to provide parts for Cultivator, all of them accepting stringent conditions of secrecy. Then the German army unleashed its blitzkrieg, which circumvented the French Maginot line and overturned the accepted military wisdom that well-manned defences could not be breached by direct assault. Hitler's flying columns had not needed any leviathan trench-digging machines. The 10 Cultivators that had been made were put into storage until the end of the war, when all but one were dismantled. Concluding his account of the episode in *The Gathering Storm*, the first volume of his history of the second world war, Churchill wrote characteristically: 'I am responsible but impenitent.'

Although the new prime minister's personal digging machine remained unused, the rest of the country greeted his arrival by excavating, as it were, in spades. 'Dig for Victory' was perhaps the most famous slogan of the second world war, and it was much more than a poster campaign. When Britain stood alone, after the fall of France and before the Nazi attack on the Soviet Union, growing more food at home was even more vital than during the 1917-18 submarine blockade. Everything imported was running low in 1941, as U-boats prowled and the transatlantic convoy system, still in its early days, struggled to cope. Between May and December 1940, perhaps the grimmest time of what was in effect a siege, a total of 3,239,190 tonnes of merchant shipping was lost, with all the vessels' cargo. Even waters close to the country's coast were so dangerous for fishermen that the price of a stone of haddock rose from a maximum of four shillings (£8.50 today) at the start of the war to 18 shillings (£30.60) by 1941. The restricted market produced occasional speciality booms, such as a dramatic demand for venison instead of hard-to-find turkey in the run-up to Christmas, but there was far too little to go round. As a trading nation, Britain was still exporting some food but with ever increasing reluctance. In December 1940, Churchill warned the United States' president, Franklin Roosevelt, that he was going to have to stop the export of 400,000 tonnes of food and fertiliser to neutral Ireland. The Irish expatriate lobby was significant in an America that Churchill was trying to bring into the war, but it was more important for Britain to eat.

Farmers' patriotism was meanwhile boosted by a subsidy of £2 for every acre of grass brought under plough. By 1944, the prewar acreages of 12m arable and 17m grass had changed to 18m and 11m, and with some approval from a traditionally conservative community. Arthur Street, a typical farmer adjusting to the change, wrote in his diary in September 1939, at the very start of the campaign: 'What a satisfactory job ploughing is. I have not personally ploughed a furrow since 1928, but I find that I have not forgotten my old skill.' His work, and that of thousands of others, paid dividends. The grand national programme of excavation brought excellent results, better than the government's most optimistic targets. In 1943 there was a record harvest; because of a growing shortage of both land and manpower, the season's target of new acres to plough had been set at 960,000 but farmers managed

1,376,000. The high ground on the Sussex downs produced its first crop since Anglo-Saxon times and the Great Park at Windsor was briefly the largest wheatfield in the country.

In the process, the mechanisation of British farming, which had been so effectively resisted during the first world war, finally proved unstoppable. Tractors and farm machinery had improved beyond measure and demand for them was insatiable. In spite of the priority given to military vehicle construction throughout the war, the number of tractors in Britain rose from 56,000 in 1939 to 70,000 the following year. By VE Day, there were 203,000. The number of disc harrows doubled between 1942 and 1946 and even the humble bicycle played a transforming role. Equipped with one, or still better a motorbike, farm labourers could travel greater distances to work and that meant less pressure on landowners to provide expensive new cottages on their farms. The tradition of 'just jiggetting along' had gone for ever and this brought a reward; farm incomes shot up between 1938 and 1943 by 207%, compared with a national average of 35%.

It was a tribute to the sophistication of the great national effort, however, that one side-effect was not forgotten. Just as the War Agricultural Committees succeeded by delegation and consulting, so the Dig for Victory campaign was prepared to allow a short but vital window of opportunity for archaeology and the beleaguered nation's history. The government even appointed a military coordinator for archaeological rescue schemes amidst all the ploughing and digging. He was Major AG Wade, whose enthusiasm derived from a famous episode at Chatham docks in 1911, when Royal Engineers digging trenches had found the remains of the earliest elephant known in Britain. Wade employed a children's school game with both soldiers and civilian volunteers, based on each pupil being encouraged to come up with a 'find'. It worked. In one air-raid trench alone he recorded – and saved for posterity – a flint sickle blade for cutting corn in the stone age, two 13th-century abbey column bases and a Norman culvert lined with medieval pottery shards. No wonder correspondents to *The Times*, such as a Mr J Morewood Dowsett, wrote to express approval and remind other excavators 'to keep an eye'.

The army meets the hunt

JANUARY 1942

A meet of the hounds for children made quite a gay scene on the village green. The master and a one-armed whip, a couple of soldiers, and some children composed the field. After having spent

Tally ho! The hunt just survives the war

the early daylight in catching and housing my few remaining mares and foals, I caught my little rough pony and joined the hunt. Hounds screamed away up into the hills. The guardians of the small ponies did gallant work in the lanes and on roads. One who had out a boy of four and a girl of five said after: 'I ran and walked with them for two-and-a-half hours. Every time I drew breath there were shouts of "Run, mummy, run!" They do not ride very well and are not strong enough to stop a pony which is gathering speed to catch up with hounds, so I have to keep a hand on each.'

The ponies are dead quiet and never 'batted an eyelash' when we got mixed up with an army convoy, tanks, lorries and goodness knows what – a high test to have an armoured car cutting in under your tail and a 'Waltzing Matilda' tank under your nose. Any hunter would have gone over the hedge into the nearest field.

Gwen McBryde

A German invader

&ↄ JANUARY 1942 ℭↄ

A herring gull came to a strange end. Its headless, freshly killed body, with a tin fastened firmly to its foot, was found on the bank of a mere. I examined it and found that the tin had been almost cut round with a tin-opener and that the flap thus made had been pushed down to its original position after the tin had been emptied. The gull had trodden on the tin, and the middle one of its three webbed toes was held fast between the side and the flap. The keeper mentioned this to some friends, one of whom said that she had seen a gull flying over Sale with what appeared to be a trap on its foot. There can be little doubt that this was the same bird, and that it had been feeding on the gulls' favourite rubbish dump at

Stretford. It had got as far as the mere, where hundreds of gulls roost, but encumbered as it was, fell prey to a fox. The same keeper also found a dead gull wearing a ring, which he gave me. The inscription *Vogelwarte Rossiten Germania* shows that it was marked at the famous ringing station on the Baltic in East Prussia, not far from Memel.

Arnold Boyd

Rabbits under siege

ℬ March 1942 ℛ

The ploughing of 23 acres of old-laid pasture has put the riverside rabbits in difficulty. Their food is gone. They have to cross 500 yards of upturned clods before they can reach the railway, beyond which lies the woodland that is the support of another colony of their kind. They have not yet adapted themselves to conditions unknown to generations of conies during more than 100 years. We surprised them at dusk on the chocolate-coloured earth the tractor has exposed to the fertilising frost. They were at a loss what to do. Caught in two minds, they ran about distractedly, some returning eventually to their strongholds in the banks of the stream and some to the railway. The immediate problem is to get food. The corn will not be sown until the end of the month. Many weeks have to pass before the oats sprout. If the conies swim the river to the big meadows on the opposite side, they will be in extremities there too. That land is also to be brought into cultivation. This will be a trying spring in many places for migrating rabbit populations.

George Muller

Menace of the sparrows

APRIL 1942

Other responsible bodies will do a public service by following the lead of the Lancashire War Agricultural Committee and encouraging the destruction of the eggs and nests of house sparrows. Sitting chirping on the eaves of the house or squabbling over some hard-won titbit in the garden, house sparrows look harmless enough, but when, in late summer, they migrate from the towns to the cornfields to feed on the ripe corn, they constitute a menace to agriculture second only to that of wood pigeons.

The same War Agricultural Committee's recent campaign against rooks raises some highly debatable questions. For though when their normal food (leatherjackets, wireworms and harmful grubs) is not available, rooks undoubtedly do attack grain and do damage, there is no evidence that the harm they do exceeds the good by so much as to justify any shooting additional to the regular shooting of the young in May, a practice itself of doubtful value.

The exposure for sale of lapwings, one of the farmer's best friends, has been reported, though not from Lancashire. The Protection of Lapwings Act (1928) forbids the sale of either the birds or their eggs between March 1 and August 31, and people who expose them for sale then render themselves liable to prosecution.

John Adams

Commando beach

JULY 2006

Seven kilometres to the east of us here at Plougasnou, by the country road there lies the tiny hamlet of Prajou. Below the settlement, a wooded valley falls steeply to the sea. The valley is now a protected nature reserve and is grazed by a pair of Highland cattle – real exotics in this warmer context – in the interest of maintaining the habitat. Halfway down the valley, a reconstructed water mill, the mill of Trobodec, a fine stone structure, is a reminder of the historic agricultural activity in the valley. But it had a more dramatic history in the years of the second world war as a memorial stone on maintained grassland near the beachhead records. The carved stone tells of the gratitude of the local community to the MTB flotillas of the Royal Navy who came into the bay under cover of darkness during winter 1944 to deliver and collect agents of the resistance network, who were active at Guimaëc.

At 10am on Wednesday I swam the high tide from the steeply shelving sandy beach that we had entirely to ourselves and I found myself contrasting my stately breaststroke on a warm summer morning with the approach of the brave young men of the Royal Navy, who would have approached this beach in darkness not sure if the shaded lights on the foreshore were the resistance – or the forces of occupation. There are plenty of other reminders of the hostilities even though this was never a major theatre of war.

On the coastal path, a German gun platform under a concrete roof, which commanded the beach at St Jean du Doigt, now enjoys the preservation as a historic site. And our local cemetery holds, under the dignified headstones of the Commonwealth War Graves Commission, the graves of five of the RAF crew of a Halifax, shot down over the coast as it flew, in 1943, from Lincolnshire to bomb the submarine pens at Lorient.

Colin Luckhurst

Ooh, country

ℬ JUNE 1942 ℭ

As I was taking some sheep to be shorn, I was joined by a very small evacuee. He said: 'You ain't got a very big flock there, but them ewe lambs is nice ones.' I asked how long he had been hereabouts. He said: 'Eighteen months, and I come from Bootle.' 'Do you like town or country best?' I asked. 'Ooh, country,' he said.

In the farmyard, a dark, gaunt, young man was shearing the heavy, floppy ewes. With his fine-cut face and his dark overall high up round his neck, he looked like a monk in a medieval manuscript. He was clipping with wonderful skill; the fleece came away in a great cloak. He said that in the past six years, he reckoned he had shorn as good as 40 acres. Farmers young and old dropped in, took a turn at the handle of the clipper and drank a glass of thin cider.

Even my triplet, bottle-fed lambs were better-grown than any there, though now, without their lambswool, they are sorry objects. If their remarks could come through they are probably saying like, the baby boy whose curls had been cut off: 'I want them on again,' which remark completed the distress of his mother.

Gwen McBryde

Pigeon pie

ℬ AUGUST 1942 ℭ

Like many others all over the country who are taking part in the British Trust inquiry into the status and habits of the wood pigeon, I have been looking for the nest of this destructive bird. Although some nests held big youngsters in the second week of May, there have been far more broods since mid-July, and whereas in spring they build in evergreens (holly, yew and fir) they now nest in any leafy tree that provides a suitable cover. In the past six weeks I have seen 13 in thorn trees, five in young firs, three in oaks, two in limes, two in a tall holly hedge, and one each in a copper beech and a flimsy elder.

We must forget their beauty and the 'livelier iris' that 'changes on the burnish'd dove' in the springtime, and must realise that they form a fifth column that is making persistent and widespread attacks on our supplies of food and fodder. And, after all, pigeon pie can be a welcome addition to our wartime diet.

Arnold Boyd

The army's coast

℘ MAY 2006 ℭ

Heading west from Marloes to Martin's Haven, the high banks are white with scurvy grass and tinted with violets. I walk down past Lockley's Lodge – where the National Trust is constructing a replica of the wooden shack built by the great Welsh naturalist in 1927. From the cove below, boats set out for Skomer, but I keep on into the deer park and out towards Wooltack Point, holding to the rim of fantastically folded and arched red cliffs all round Mouse's Haven.

I peer down, and catch one of the magical sights of these western coasts – the black cross/white cross flicker of a Manx shearwater careening along the wave troughs, the epitome of urgent grace. It reminds me of Caroline, the shearwater Ronald Lockley gave to the conductor of the Boston Symphony Orchestra in the 1930s. The latter took her by plane to Boston and released her; the postcard he then sent Lockley arrived a week after Caroline's return to Skokholm, the little island south of Skomer where Lockley lived from 1927 until the war, when the MoD forced him (and others along the finest stretch of limestone coastline in Britain, on what are now the Castlemartin tank ranges) to leave. Fate was kinder to Skokholm, and it became a nature reserve.

Clouds of gulls rise from the great stack of the Mew Stone by Skomer, trailing a small fishing boat. Puffins are rafting up in the lee of the island. A seal slips out of one of the caves in the cove beneath me. I round the headland, look towards Druidstone and Newgale, and see three tankers moored within the marine nature reserve, no doubt waiting to head in to the oil jetties of Milford Haven.

Jim Perrin

All hands to the harvest

ᖚ SEPTEMBER 1942 ᖙ

Every hand the farmer could spare was sent by car today to a 30-acre field, the first in the district to be ploughed and the first to be cut, to resite the stooks of oats. At a casual glance, you would have thought the heavy crop was wasted. Here and there corn was sprouting in the sheaves, some of the stooks had been blown over and had lain for days on end in shallow watercourses scooped by floods, and every butt was a sodden mass that looked as though it could never be dried. The headman shook his head over the mess the crop was in, but as the wind grew sharper and the sun shone stronger, he began to eat the doleful words he had let fall at '10 o'clocks'. 'Maybe it won't be so bad after all. If the sun and wind go on doing their best it'll soon be time to turn over the butts to dry. I think we may get a tonne an acre out of this lot. It's terribly hard work; we haven't enough men to go round. I'll gamble fellows in the south country don't work half as hard as we do here.'

Ronald Garnett

Picking the flowers

I was recently given copies of *Wild Flower Magazine* for 1939-1946, which contain a wonderful series of cameos of botanists at war. This was the journal of the Wild Flower Society, presided by Edith Dent until her death in 1948. Edith's vigorous editorials reflect the society's practical war effort, with calls to the membership to send sphagnum moss to Red Cross depots, for use as wound dressings. Some issues contain advice on collecting rosehips and medicinal herbs including foxglove leaves, which fetched 95 shillings a hundredweight in 1940. Members' botanical activities consisted of competitively collecting plant records, which they submitted in diaries to local branches. At the height of the Battle of Britain come joyful reports of new discoveries of sea holly on what might soon become invasion beaches. There are complaints, too, about members being interrogated as spies and about petrol rationing. Long motoring jaunts hunting rare species were impossible, so competition for collections within a five-mile radius of home became popular. In Christmas 1940, the Scottish secretary reports that his branch diaries narrowly escaped destruction when a landmine crashed through his outhouse roof without exploding. Members' letters make especially poignant reading. Apologies for not submitting diaries come from Sgt Grieves, who lost his in the retreat from Dunkirk, and from the grief-stricken sister-in-law of the Captain of HMS Courageous, an early naval casualty. The strongest impression on rereading these magazines is that natural history provided members with genuine solace from the horrors of war.

Phil Gates

Mossy medicine

ဆာ SEPTEMBER 1942 ၥ

Any day that is unfit for carrying corn I snatch to collect sphagnum moss from the moor. Thousands of swabs and stretcher pillows are being sent to the Middle East and there is no stock in London from which to draw for hospitals at home. The moss contains iodine and is four times more absorbent than cotton wool. It has wonderful healing and aseptic qualities and can be used at the forward dressing stations without being sterilised. It was discovered by accident by the Germans in the last war. Some wounded soldiers were unable to move to a first-aid dressing station and they gathered some sphagnum moss to stop bleeding. They used it as pads and tied their handkerchiefs round it. When a doctor examined their wounds four days later, he expected to find gangrene, but found the wounds clean and beginning to heal.

The moss should be collected before winter as it cannot be dried by artificial heat. It is best to leave it a few days in a heap on the moor when you gather it, to dry. Then it can be brought down and the bits of reed and pine needles picked out. It should then be sent to the nearest central supply depot or direct to Lady Boynton, 41 Lowndes Square, London SW.

Gwen McBryde

Heavy breathing

ဆာ OCTOBER 1942 ၥ

A stranger came to my yard one evening, and I found him searching an empty shippon for the pig whose stertorous breathing he thought he could hear. I have given up pig-keeping because of the shortage

160

of foodstuffs, and wondered for a moment if the spectre of Sally, the sow who reared so many big litters, had come back to the scene of her triumphs. The mystery was soon solved when a barn owl entered the loft with a mouse in its talons, to be greeted with loud snores from its grateful youngsters. At night, when all is quiet, this snoring continues by the hour and may be heard at some distance. A friend of mine who came to live in a country house where a pair of barn owls had a nest was equally misled; for some time he thought it was his housekeeper!

Arnold Boyd

The Nazi toadstool plot

ॐ OCTOBER 1997 ॐ

What has turned into a rather promising toadstool season has produced clusters of puffballs all over my wood. Most seem to be the pear-shaped fruiting bodies – rarely any bigger than golf balls – of *Lycoperdon perlatum* and *Lycoperdon pyriforme*, perhaps the species Dryden was thinking of in his line, 'My Phyllis me with pelted puff-ball plies'. Small they may be, but when they are ripe, they contain billions of spores, which are released through a hole in the top of the ball like puffs of smoke whenever it is disturbed by gusts of wind or raindrops. Hence the now sadly defunct names 'puckfist', 'puffe's fist' or 'fist balls' – 'fist' being vernacular for fart. Alas, there are no giant puffballs, which, as well as growing to sizes and spore-masses that make them probably the most prolific organisms on the planet, are one of the most delectable to eat. Famous giants include a five-foot-diameter specimen reported from New York State in 1877, and mistaken at a distance for a sheep, and one found under an oak tree in Kent during the second world war, initially believed to be a

German secret weapon. Most specimens are between six inches and a foot in diameter, but even these can be an embarrassment to pickers, as there is a limit to the number of fried, sweetbread-tasting slices you can eat. (Victorian fungophiles had a novel solution, leaving the ball in situ and hacking off slices on a cut-and-come-again basis.) In Suffolk, a rare relative of the puffballs continues to thrive on the sandy roadside by Blyford church, where I chanced on it in 1973. *Battarraea phalloides* is an extraordinary toadstool. A long, fibrous stalk carries a brown puffball-like sac on its top. This splits round the rim to expose the spores, which lurk inside the cap like a thick layer of rust.

© *Richard Mabey*

Birds and bombs

℘ DECEMBER 1942 ℛ

War is bringing changes to the wildlife of the country. The appearance of an unusual bird or of abnormal numbers in times of active war will always be attributed to conditions abroad by those who seek an easy explanation. The fact is that disturbance caused by actual fighting and bombing is of very limited effect. One spring morning I went at daybreak to the craters made by a landmine and a big bomb during the night. By one a greenfinch went up and down in wavy breeding flight; on the lip of the larger crater a willow-wren sang its territorial song. Their alarm was short-lived.

It is rather the change in agriculture (which we hope will be permanent) and in game-preserving that brings about corresponding changes in the wild birds' status. I feared that last winter's widespread laying and cutting of the tall hedges, as arable replaced pasture, would drive away many of our turtledoves, and such was the case; never in the past 20 summers have I seen so few near my home. There are far fewer pheasants, for none are hand-reared now, but magpies, jays and crows flourish as never before. Foxes have been shot (though one took three of my pullets recently), but rats abound in the numerous wheatstacks. I was present with my terrier when a stack was threshed, and found old rats, half-grown and quite small ones together. One took refuge inside the trouser leg of a farm labourer, who was less amused than his fellow-workers.

Arnold Boyd

The big metal hawks

ℰↃ DECEMBER 1942 ℃ℛ

Birds, like ourselves, are rapidly becoming accustomed to aircraft (we may no longer call them aeroplanes), and seem hardly to notice what they once took for huge hawks. It was a very different state of things a few years ago. The geese and ducks in my orchard shot into their houses if an aircraft passed over; now they only look up. Not many years ago every duck of some 3,000 on a big reservoir in the Midlands flew high into the sky in their excitement when an aircraft passed the pool at a considerable height; and they took a long time to settle down again. Now it is only low-flying aircraft that cause even a mild alarm; a few duck, it is true, flew up when one skimmed the surface of the mere close to them a few days ago, but even they returned to the water at once, and the rest paid no heed whatever. Some bombing ranges, so I am told, have been deserted by the geese that normally winter there, but in others, to my own knowledge, the effect of intermittent bombing is more than counterbalanced by the fact that fishermen and ramblers keep clear of such places, and the duck enjoy more peace than they have for years.

Some of us remember the days when horses would hardly face a motor car, even when a red flag led the way. 'Custom reconciles us to everything.'

Arnold Boyd

A diarist's own adventure

ℰ JANUARY 2000 ℛ

As a new year dawned, a milestone one, we took our dogs and our sticks to walk in the Cheviots. Reaching the car park at Ingram we were into snow and, thankfully abandoning our vehicle, set off up the hills. All-terrain bikes had blazed a trail, because shepherds here do their rounds on wheels now rather than legs. Times have changed: two feet are no longer enough with one man having to look after three hirsels – these are hills hosting 500 sheep. Almost all lambing is done in hemmels and when the lambs are a few days old, provided they are fit, families are turned out.

The greatest drawback to the motorised accomplice is that it prevents the shepherd hearing his sheep, so they still use collies. A good dog, with a sharp sense of smell, can find sheep overblown by snow. A ewe can live several days in an igloo-type cave with air filtering through tiny air holes in the snow. The collie will seek out these vents, caused by the ascending breath of entombed beasts, and sniff the warm sheep-scent, barking to bring the shepherd when he has success. During the second world war, an American plane crashed in a blizzard in the heathery slopes on Cheviot. With my father, I joined the shepherd's party searching for survivors in a fearful snow-storm – I cannot imagine why I was allowed to tag along, I was a child, but I have not forgotten the adventure.

It was a shepherd's dog that went up the slopes of a steep, marshy ghyll and found the crashed plane and four injured airmen. This collie bitch was subsequently awarded the Dickin medal for animal bravery. At one time, the majority of rescue dogs were alsatians, now they are mainly border collies, which are trained by the Search and Rescue Dog Association.

The Northern Upland Moorland Regeneration Project has just launched a scheme to regenerate 3,600 hectares of moorland near Bellingham, to bring benefits to the local economy and wildlife. Six farms have been given business appraisals and cattle houses will be built to take animals off the moor during winter. If the red grouse thrive here, as they once did, this will enable 14 square miles to be used as a shooting moor, providing cash inflow and seasonal jobs.

Veronica Heath

V-sign in the sky

℘ DECEMBER 1942 ℘

In this part of the country we see many 'Victory' signs in the sky. Most frequently the V is composed of common gulls returning to the coast at sunset, less often of a skein of geese moving from place to place, and on rare occasions of a herd of swans. Yesterday, when searching among a group of cress beds for water-rails, snipe and other marshland birds, I heard what I thought was the call of travelling geese. It was not long, however, before I realised my mistake, when out of the northern haze a large white V appeared, moving across a clear blue sky, a herd of Bewick's swans. The birds were flying at so great a height that the winter sun lit up their underparts, and to the naked eye the skein resembled a piece of white silk ribbon fluttering in the wind. With the glass it was possible to see that their necks were relatively short, and their calls, pitched on a single note, made it certain that they were Bewick's and not whooper swans. It must have been upwards of five minutes from the time when they appeared till they were lost to view again in the south-west. There were 39, and when I first saw them, one leg of the V was twice as long as the other. When they reached a point nearly overhead, they changed formation and for a moment became a rabble, but soon reformed to a perfect V, and so they passed from sight, leaving a memory that will not quickly be forgotten.

Ronald Garnett

CHAPTER EIGHT

TURNING THE TIDE

Some of the lowest moments for the countryside during the second world war came at irregular intervals when rationing supplies suffered a hiccup and the local pub would put up a sign, unimaginable in today's times of plenty, saying 'No beer.' This happened often enough during the early years of rationing for outside visitors to report resentment on top of the usual rural caution if they called at a village pub and asked for a full pint. Curious alternative brews were one remedy, and there was much experimenting with 'natural' beers and wines based on countryside plants, sometimes with the unwitting help of the government. Lord Woolton's Food Ministry was a constant source of innovative cooking ideas, helped by a panel of 24 female volunteers from across the country, who advised civil servants on their own clever ways at home in villages or towns with rationed food. One result was Lord Woolton Pie, a concoction of cauliflowers, carrots, swedes, spring onions, parsley, oatmeal and the minister's own great favourite, potatoes. Another was a booklet called *The Hedgerow Harvest*, which revealed the astonishing larder available from wild plants. This played a part, in turn, in the formation of County Herb Committees, whose volunteers picked more than 4,000 tonnes of medicinal plants to help the war effort. It also alerted some to the number of intoxicants on their doorstep. There was nothing cosier, if the pub was shut, than to curl up with a glass of elderberry wine or nettle beer.

Nettles were a subject of great rural interest during the war. Mrs KH Rees-Mogg, a forebear of the *Times'* editor William Rees-Mogg, started a discussion in *Country Life* magazine about how much of the plant should be used for various supplements to the ration. 'The question has been raised by my cook, whose nettle soup I have found to be excellent, preferring it to spinach,' she wrote. The particular problem was how far down the stem from the nettle's top the Rees-Moggs' cook should go when snipping off leaves to use for nettle tea. Dandelions also came into their own, alongside vegetables new to most dinner tables, such as the globe artichoke and broccoli, an American favourite whose cultivation spread in villages near US army bases in the months before D-Day on 6 June 1944. American 'GI' general infantrymen might sometimes be sneered at as 'over-sexed, over-paid and over here', but they were also welcome guests in households where gifts from their camps' stores were exotic, chocolate especially.

The constant difficulties of making do with limited supplies made villagers very aware of waste and a 'green' approach to using everything and then re-using it, familiar to today's recycling world, took hold. It was fostered by the government, which passed regulations forbidding the destruction of paper, cardboard and bones, all of which could be reused or had alternative uses – boiled-down bones provided glue for aircraft production as well as glycerine for explosives. Parish councils were instructed to designate a central collecting point for the material, partly to foster a spirit of communal work for the war just as today's recycling centres, in supermarket car parks or on office forecourts, tend to be prominently sited. Many who lived through the period recall the feeling of virtue as a week's supply of the *Manchester Guardian* (itself sometimes limited to six pages because of paper rationing) or a pile of cardboard boxes was dumped on the pile. Kitchen waste was also centrally collected for animal feed, a programme encouraged by slogans from Lord Woolton's tireless department, such as: 'Beat the enemy in your own kitchen. Put your reply to Hitler's threats in the waste food bin.' More famously, it became a mark of patriotism to have had iron railings removed for supposed reforging into tank armour or to donate aluminium saucepans and kettles in the belief that they would be turned into parts for Spitfires. Much of the collected metal proved useless and was dumped in the English Channel, but the minister for aircraft production, Lord Beaverbrook, considered the drive a public relations success. He was helped by radio broadcasts of songs such as one on the new life of a housewife's kettle:

My saucepans have all been surrendered
The teapot is gone from the hob
The colander's leaving the cabbage
For a very much different job.

So now, when I hear on the wireless
Of Hurricanes showing their mettle
I see in a vision before me
A Dornier chased by my kettle.

The communal fervour was increased when cases of official profligacy came to light, reviving the village tradition of sniping at 'little Hitlers' with too strong a sense of their own importance. The army was forced to hold an inquiry into lax standards at its temporary camps near the Channel coast after the rescue of the British Expeditionary Force from Dunkirk in June 1940. A farmer collecting waste for pigswill found, in just one large bucket, six uncut loaves, two packets of butter and dozens of uncooked sausages, known in army slang as 'dead babies' legs'. No one thought that the evacuated troops were anything but heroes, but such lax use of scarce resources caused outrage. Parliament appointed a Committee on Waste five months later and regulations were tightened up.

Snitching on ordinary offenders, as opposed to army canteen managers, was not part of countryside culture. The whole, grand system of keeping illegal secret pigs would have collapsed had that been so. But the suspicion deliberately fostered during the invasion scares of 1940-1 lasted for the whole war and produced some surprising, temporary customs. John and David Fairhall, who were both later to serve with distinction as *Guardian* journalists, were then boys, and their parents ran a post office. The household was issued with a kettle, presumably not aluminium, to use for steaming open 'suspicious' post as well as making tea. The study of letters at a village post office had all sorts of fascinations. Sweethearts in the forces pioneered the system of 'initial messages' on envelopes such as SWALK (sealed with a loving kiss) and the more bawdy NORWICH and SIAM. The angle at which a stamp had been placed was a sign of varying degrees of suggestiveness or passion.

For much of the time, however, most people were simply too busy for snooping or meddling gratuitously in others' business. Apart from family and jobs, enormous efforts went into do-it-yourself methods of making spartan daily life more comfortable. In spite of severe droughts in 1940 and 1941, and a washout year for gardening in 1944, allotments burgeoned. From 815,000 in 1939 the national total rose to 1,400,000 in four years. Poultry and pig-keeping came close to toppling fishing from its time-honoured position as the country's favourite hobby. By the end of the war, a quarter of all eggs eaten came from domestic pet hens. There were 6,900 Pig Clubs, which shared everything from rearing tips to swill, and the Domestic Poultry Keepers' Council recorded an all-time record total of more than 1,250,000 members.

Finally, there were the pests. The conversion of so much land and so many people to crop cultivation led to a sudden awareness that rabbits and mice might not be just the innocuous cast of Beatrix Potter tales after all. Controversy raged in the *Guardian*'s Country Diary, as elsewhere, over whether targeted species of birds, especially pigeons, rooks and sparrows, were to be condemned as grain thieves or praised as destroyers of much more damaging insect pests. Carrier pigeons complicated the issue, and there was further spirited debate when the Air Ministry suggested that the birds' predators, hawks and falcons, should be shot on sight. The *Guardian*'s editor, William Crozier, bridled at another government demand that sparrows and their nests should be 'destroyed by all and sundry', an edict not to be equalled in severity until Chairman Mao ordered everyone in China to kill sparrows in the 1950s. One of Crozier's deputies, JL Hammond, was incensed that evacuee children enlisted to hunt for, and wreck, nests in his village near Manchester had ' ... of course, destroyed everything'. The ministries, however, remained implacable and when the hunt for extra ploughing land reached right up to river banks where water rats and voles had their burrows, that countryside icon, Ratty was added to the list of approved targets.

The fire watchers' otter

ଔ JANUARY 1943 ର

An hour or so before snow began to fall we saw, as we left the fire watchers' post in a timber yard, an otter running along a wall above a big, deep dam. He was in no hurry, so we had plenty of time to notice how this water weasel arches his back while on land in much the same way as he humps it up in the act of submerging. Of this characteristic of his gait we never tire. Next morning we were early at the riverside looking for tracks. The otter had visited the drain and had crossed a narrow tongue of land to gain the river. For once in a way he had omitted to indulge in a roll on the grass. Footings of other creatures were much more interesting. Especially those of a heron, who had pronged with his feet the banks of the mill lade for a distance of a hundred yards. What he had been up to we did not discover. There was no evidence of a kill of fish or small rodent. The tramway lines of rabbits were all over the place. They gave the show away badly for the conies. The trapper visited their burrows and took 15 with his ferret and nets.

Gwen McBryde

Taking novel menus too far

ଔ JANUARY 1943 ର

A second visit to the flooded vale was made this week under less pleasant conditions, but proved of greater interest to the bird-watcher, for several new species of ducks had arrived and a single adult whooper swan had joined the family party of five Bewicks. Perhaps 'joined' is the wrong word, for although this bird was on the same sheet of water it showed no interest in the other swans, though like them it allowed me to approach quite closely, uttering now and then a single note of disapproval. In addition to the vast number of ducks, there were hundreds of lapwings and golden plover to be seen. These plovers are usually scattered in flocks over the fields, but when the moon is full they feed at night and spend the day in comparative idleness. So at least we used to think in Norfolk, where there were greater opportunities of observation. Several black-backed gulls had come inland from the coast, and with them an immature glaucous gull, a species that winters on this coast but rarely leaves the sea. A few days later a farmer whose home is on the river bank told me that his boy had shot two goosanders and two black divers, which were evidently shags. He had made presents of them to his friends, but if they have eaten them they will perhaps be friends no longer.

Ronald Garnett

The threat of slicks

✌ MARCH 1943 ✌

I was summoned hurriedly to see a strange bird in a ploughed field near my home, and found a badly oiled common gull walking about slowly and occasionally picking up food. Its breast was dark brown and the stain extended up its neck and stopped just below its eyes. It was little wonder that the cyclist who first saw and reported it took it for some little-known species. Before the war the amount of waste oil discharged into the sea was serious enough; in present conditions this menace to bird life must increase – a bad outlook for birds such as the guillemot and scoter, which spend the winter at sea.

The change from grassland to arable continues. I watch a tractor ploughing a steep bank of old turf in a park that only necessity and a War Agricultural Committee could disturb, and another of the few remaining thorn hedges, which surrounded many a pasture, has been cut down to the ground. As I expected when all this ploughing began, partridges have increased considerably, and a farming friend reports the same elsewhere in Cheshire; but the loss of the big thorn fences will further reduce our turtledoves this summer.

On the last day of February, the earliest date on which I have seen them, bright meadow pipits had reached the meadows where I look for them each spring. These clean birds (the few that winter here become shabby in plumage) usually arrive late in March – our first summer immigrants.

Arnold Boyd

Cocks and tits

ഇഉ APRIL 1943 ൗ

Window-tapping by birds attracted (or, more properly, excited) by their own reflections, to which I have referred in a recent Country Diary, has been paralleled by the action of a barn-door cock that MH of Bolton watched in a Welsh farmyard. It attacked the panels of a police car (which must have been better polished than the majority one sees today), and with its hackles raised hurled itself repeatedly at the side of the car. I hardly think, however, that the crouching attitude that it assumed from time to time meant that it was looking under the car for its rival, but rather that this was the position that a cock takes up when attacking.

SC of London asks for information about the habit that blue tits have formed of piercing, and sometimes removing, the cardboard caps of milk bottles and drinking the contents. This habit seems to be widespread and to have been acquired independently in many different places. My correspondent wonders whether the trick in fact spread from one pioneer who first discovered this sort of food, and hopes to learn when the habit was first reported in various localities. The earliest date of which he has knowledge is 1936 or 1937, but I have an idea that similar attacks were made some time before that. I remember my neighbours' indignation when blue tits first started on their bottles years ago. This was in the country, but urban tits sometimes visit us and the trick may have been learned elsewhere. Although not regarded as migrant birds, blue tits undoubtedly wander about the country a great deal.

Arnold Boyd

The plough and the hounds

   ₨ MAY 1943 ₩

The influence that the greater cultivation of the soil is having on the sport of hound trailing, flourishing in the mountain and foothill country as never before, is something that none of us anticipated. The race is to the strong. Only hounds of robust physique can stand up to the gruelling travelling for between 30 and 40 minutes over land consisting so largely of plough. Brains, speed and determination in finishing still count for a good deal, but it is the stamina of big-boned hounds that overrides all. Trail hounds, as everybody with any knowledge of the driving of the scent of aniseed and turpentine is aware, are descended from the mountain foxhounds. But for many years there has been much inbreeding, with the result that a large number of hounds, especially those that are entered chiefly in the low country trails, have degenerated and become whippety in appearance. Plough, even more than crag, scree, and bracken, tests the bone and muscle of trail hounds, and we are noting the success of those that are the more nearly related to the hounds that kill their foxes in the high fells. How they will fare when hot weather arrives is, however, another matter.

George Muller

The Italians arrive

℘ MAY 1943 ℧

An added complication on the farm is the advent of six Italian prisoner workers. They are doing very well, but what with chatting of this and that and some getting their feet wet and others wanting flowers, time is needed to deal with them.

I visited today a farm bought by two young men. They have lost a good deal of their recently acquired stock, and I fear they will have more of what my old woodman called 'unlucky misfortunes'. He used to describe the misdoings of a 'yow' (ewe) he owned who would start at the tail and eat her way up the lamb. I notice no result from my ability to find four-leaved clovers, or fives or sixes if put to it. When I used to give them to my companions they seemed uncertain if the luck was transferable. I consulted a learned man who knew everything. He was always intensely shy of giving his opinion but murmured something about 'the seeing eye', and I think that's about all the luck there is in it.

Gwen McBryde

An armistice for quails

℘ MAY 1943 ℧

The call 'wet-my-lips' from a wheatfield caught my ear as I was passing along a country lane – the call notes of a quail. I have heard this bird only once before in Cheshire, and the sound took me back to the fields of France and to the south of Spain, where we heard many on the rough, wide pastures where the great bustards live. The war may quite possibly help this species, for quails used to be netted in thousands on the North African coast to please the gourmets of Europe. Great numbers pass through Egypt. I have watched weary birds just topping the waves as they arrived on the Sinai coast in autumn, and could well understand the ease with which the hungry Israelites captured them during their desert wanderings. 'Shoot-a da quail' is often the suggestion of the touting dragoman in Cairo.

The quail may possibly breed here, but other migrants that do not stay are still passing through the county. Six sanderlings, birds that seldom come inland except during May on their way to the Arctic, were flying over the Flashes on Tuesday, and yesterday a fine black tern was catching flies over the mere, beating up and down with its characteristic dipping flight.

Arnold Boyd

Wild flowers in peril

ℬ May 1943 ℭ

Cottage gardens seem to be in much better form this year than the bigger flower gardens. In this prolific season, strong-growing plants are smothering their more delicate neighbours, and one cannot do much life-saving – there is no time. Night-scented stocks and sweet rockets in one small garden I passed were scenting the air. Growing amongst them was love-in-a-mist, and I was pleased to see the common white pink, which is so much nicer, I think, than the grander Mrs Simpkins and is becoming quite a rare plant.

Ploughing up has killed off so many of the rarer wild flowers. Most of the orchis tribe seem likely to go, except those that grow in woods or on moors. I still know a corner of a small grass field where a white-scented orchis grows, and on some blocks of stone on the moor above, the bright purple saxifrage makes a close-growing carpet. I have never been able to make this plant last many seasons in my garden – it always disappears. Ants killed my last patch; they made a nest under it. Roots and early kale have suffered badly from fly. The dry early season has suited the insect world only too well.

Gwen McBryde

Swallows in the trenches

ஐ June 1943 ஐ

An energetic friend climbed to a kestrel's nest in a big beech tree. It contained four eggs, and round the rim of the nest were a number of pellets of indigestible matter, which the bird had ejected as it sat on its eggs. I sent seven of these pellets to a friend at the museum, who identified the remains of at least two long-tailed fieldmice and a common shrew and found that several of the pellets contained only fur. Here we have further proof of the kestrel's value to the farmer, and yet I know an otherwise intelligent keeper who shoots every kestrel he sees and (directly contrary to the law) any tawny or barn owl he can find; and this because a very young pheasant or partridge has occasionally been picked up by these birds. It is his employer who is really to blame for not insisting that the law should be kept.

A pair of swallows have aroused great interest in the village school by building a nest in the air-raid shelter in the playground, just as other pairs built in dugouts in France during the last war. The village boys assure me that it will be as carefully protected as were those 25 years ago, when the nests were in some cases signed for along with other trench stores by relieving troops.

Arnold Boyd

Parcel post

I know a lovely bend in the river Wye where steep rocks go down to the water. There are fine pools for salmon, and you can find a sheltered corner for a dip. Large clumps of chives grow on the rocks; they are in bloom and almost as pretty as thrift. I grow them as an edging in my kitchen garden. They are compact and neat and very useful in salads for flavouring. Wild garlic grows in the woods here, and I have planted a yellow-flowered variety, but garlic is not popular in England.

I am besieged by people wanting strawberries. I like to provide the village jam-makers as far as possible and particularly the visitors who come from towns to stay in our village shop. It is now the hub of our universe. Before the war it was almost completely neglected except by children wanting sweets or by some folk who had become used to the large white cottage loaves baked there. Now it is promoted to be a post office. Previously the kind owner of the shop used to suggest, after much trying of weights and pondering over parcels, that perhaps we had better leave the decision to the postman when he called.

Gwen McBryde

A talented land girl

There is a curious chill in the air, much appreciated by the animals after their fly-tormented days. Hay-making is going on steadily. On one part of the farm, a gallant effort was made getting in a fodder crop on the steep slope of Broomy Hill, slippery oats and heavy peas. One man and a wonderful boy of 12 and a girl worked from morning until 10pm. The slight, fair girl drove the tractor – not everyone's job with heavy loads to turn on the slippery banks, but she has flown aeroplanes, was a fine cross-country rider and has driven ambulances in the blitz. The middle-aged women are doing admirable work, and one 'over-60' is chafing at having to stay in to look after a farmer's children while his wife is in hospital.

The under-school-age children accompany their mothers; some of the small boys manage to get themselves taken on the tractor and fall asleep – gassed, I think – but they will be there. One, who was poking a stick about in the hay, was heard to remark, referring to my bailiff: 'Do you think if I kept on at this hours and hours, he'd give me something? I haven't had a bob out of him so far.'

Gwen McBryde

An evacuee chooses to stay

ಬಿ JULY 1943 ಧ

The village school broke up this week and the little boys arrive in couples 'to help'. They choose their farm and remain there firmly until given a job. The evacuee boy of eight or nine refused to be taken home; he was somewhat shaken when his family returned to the station in tears, but he remained at the farm. His speciality is sheep; he manages to be in at all dipping and shearing, and appears to have been in charge of the hand-reared lambs at the farm where he lives.

I have seen one field of wheat cut and, of course, oats, some of it laid rather badly; a lot of barley has gone down. Beans are good and we are cutting them now. Jays have destroyed all my garden peas and the broad beans. Chiffchaffs seem to be busy in the peas too. Last night I watched some willow wrens enjoying themselves amongst the flowers in a herbaceous border. Magpies are increasing terribly; it is impossible to spare cartridges to shoot them, and they sit and watch by any hen who lays out and then eat the egg the moment she leaves her nest.

Gwen McBryde

A chink in the blackout

ཀྀ AUGUST 1943 ཀྀ

It was like old times to have lights on before it was necessary to draw the curtains. I like to see moths buzz up to the windows and stare in with their eyes like motor headlights, and I dislike losing touch with what is going on outside. There is always a chance that a gate

Dippersmoor Manor, the 12th–17th century farm of Gwen McBryde

has been left open or that an enterprising cow has broken into a wood or cornfield. I like to see bats hunting up and down or an owl float out of the orchard.

Already there are long furrows ploughed in the lower meadow, which has been grass so long that no one can remember it otherwise. In fact, I am told that it was cut every year for hay owing to the colchicum or meadow saffron, which made it dangerous for grazing. 'Old Dan'l', a retired farmer, told me how he and three men cut the 25 acres with scythes in a week; his wife used the whetstone and brought their food. After all this haymaking the grass took some bringing round. No doubt ploughing up now will do it no harm.

Gwen McBryde

The Home Guard's beast

෨ SEPTEMBER 1943 ෬

A friend, returning from Home Guard duties at half-past 10 o'clock, saw ahead of him in the country lane a creature going all out to avoid being overtaken. The lights of the car were sufficient to enable the motorist to see that the beast was neither fox, otter, rabbit, hare, cat nor dog, but what other animal it was, the driver could not determine. The car was running in top gear, the speed was increased from 22 miles to almost 30 miles an hour, yet for 230 yards – the distance was measured next morning – the fugitive kept ahead. The gait was no clue to the identity of the hunted. In an otter the arched back and the bounding attitude, and in a fox the long brush held straight out, would have sufficed for the clearing up of the mystery. But when suddenly the animal broke right-handed for the hedge, the dalesman knew at once what it was that was afoot. The striped head and the long pointed muzzle could belong only to a badger, and a badger, moreover, not more than a quarter of a mile away from a colony on a fellside just outside the village. The Home Guard officer, a man in his late 50s, has lived in the district all his life, he has hunted since he was a boy, but this was the first time he had set eyes on a badger about on his lawful business.

George Muller

Italy calls it a day

ℰ SEPTEMBER 1943 ℭ

Foxes had an exciting time during the harvest and were very noisy at night. Wire netting is almost unobtainable, and so more fowls than ever wander free and are carried off by 'Mr Reynolds', to use the farmhand's phrase. A local master of hounds lost some pullets; it reminds one of the man who burgled Scotland Yard. And so the farmers took their opportunity. One man carried a shotgun across his knees as he drove his tractor and shot two foxes as they left the corn. There is a corpse on a fence in an oatfield near my house; its brush is gone, no doubt as a trophy.

There were more turtledoves in the fields yesterday afternoon than we have seen all summer; an hour or two later came the news of Italy's surrender.

Arnold Boyd

Everyone pitches in

ℰ OCTOBER 1943 ℭ

Yesterday, when the sun shone there were demands that ladders should be reared against the branches of old pear trees laden with small, sweet fruit. There is no dearth of wasps here on the fallen split pears. Admiral and small tortoiseshell butterflies visit them too. The stone stile makes a convenient resting place for the very small boys, who sit there munching and watching the sheep-dipping. A four-year-old child was cracking nuts with his teeth with the ease of a squirrel, while a busy eight-year-old fellow, wearing a protective kilt of old sacking tied with string round his waist, drove down the ewe lambs to the dipping shed. Women came by with a lorry-load of rakings from the stubbles, and a little way off a caterpillar tractor ploughed up and down a steep bank, while on the level a little boy was driving a tractor and liming a field.

I bought some prize-winning ewe lambs and next day found them infested with maggots; these creatures develop with dreadful rapidity. The old saying about losing a sheep for a ha'porth of tar was not unfounded.

Gwen McBryde

Dad's Army and the geese

໔ OCTOBER 1943 ໕

One night towards the end of September, two watchers at a small observatory were startled from their star-gazing by a noise like the baying of hounds. Recognising it after their first surprise as the honking of geese, they looked up and saw about 20 flying in a perfect V across the face of the moon. These geese seem to have taken up their quarters somewhere in the neighbourhood. Two nights ago, Home Guards on patrol saw them flying over, and early yesterday morning they passed over, little more than tree top high. In the afternoon I searched the most likely places for them but failed to find them.

Those who have seen them agree they are not Canada geese, several pairs of which breed along the Thames not far away and doubtless wander about the surrounding country together in autumn and winter, and it looks as if they are some sort of grey geese. And if the date on which they were first seen is anything to go by, they are probably pinkfoots, which reach us in some numbers in September. Whitefronts rarely arrive before the beginning of October, and I know of none having been seen in the part of Berkshire south of the Thames before the middle of October.

John Adams

A merry prisoner

ᔧ OCTOBER 1943 ᔥ

I am told that it is a vintage year for hops in these parts. Today I was taken round a hopyard where the last day's work was in full swing. The owner showed me the golden resin inside each petal of a flowerhead. It is this that is wanted for the brewing of beer. Pale green trusses were being torn down and women and children were stripping off the flowers into canvas cradles. A man with a basket measure came to each cradle when it was full and measured the hops. A merry Italian prisoner seemed to be enjoying driving a loaded wagon off to the drying buildings. He was obviously from the south. I spoke to him and he chattered away. I fancy he thought hops a poor affair after the white grapes of Italy.

I went on to see the drying process, expecting to see a kiln, but there was nothing like that. I mounted a stair into a long, dim room where piles of hops lay, some still hot, just tipped off the big trays that had been brought from the ovenlike compartments behind shuttered doors along one side of the room. Sulphur fumes mixed with the pungent smell of baked hops.

Gwen McBryde

Send for the Scouts

ℰ OCTOBER 1943 ℜ

As I came home at daybreak today (thanks to a night's Civil Defence duty) the advent of winter was obvious. Black against the brightening sky, it was the cones and catkins of the alder that impressed, although most ash trees are still holding many of their pinnate leaves. The elm's twisted branches were clearly outlined against the sky but, characteristically, the beech is clinging to its bronzed leaves. Poplar, horse-chestnut and lime are completely bare, whilst the birch and sycamore still retain a few terminal leaves.

I was annoyed to find fresh evidence of indiscriminate hacking and chopping of young silver birches on the slopes of 'my' valley. The education of our youth seems to be still incomplete in this respect, and it is to be hoped that in the postwar Britain now being planned, a place will be found for lessons on the social duty of preservation. Farmers here can hardly be blamed for their reluctance to work the Home Timber Production Department's scheme for removing dead wood and trees through the agency of the Boy Scouts, so long as there are so many hooligans about who have not the benefit of the Scouts' training.

BA

Sticking up for pigeons

ℰ NOVEMBER 1943 ℜ

One so seldom hears a word spoken in favour of wood pigeons that an instance of their doing good seems worth recording. Last summer, a schoolboy correspondent of mine shot a wood pigeon on a farm in the Chilterns and found its crop half full not of wheat, as might have been expected from the prevalence of shocked wheat hereabouts, but of woodlice, between 30 and 40 in all. He adds that he has often seen wood pigeons pecking at wood on the ground, so it seems unlikely that the one he shot was an isolated benefactor.

Another schoolboy tells me that he saw a long-eared owl in a fir wood in southern Berkshire last summer. It was sitting close to the trunk of a tree with its 'ears' erect, as long-eared owls do, so there seems no doubt it was one. This is the first I have heard of from Berkshire for some time. Eight or ten years ago I was told by keepers that several frequented fir woods on the Downs in winter, but I never found any at the places they mentioned. Oxfordshire seems to have been abandoned altogether by long-eared owls. Fifty years ago a few used to nest in spinneys in the north of the county, but nowadays you will look for one there in vain.

John Adams

A banned coast

ℬ NOVEMBER 1943 ℭ

When opportunities for bird-watching on the North Riding coast are few, it is pleasant to come across a sea-bird far inland, especially when the wanderer has not died from exhaustion or been shot because it is a stranger. Three days ago, a neighbour came running to tell me she had caught a little bird, and when I lifted the upturned basin that covered it I found, as I expected from her description, that it was a little auk. How it reached her tiny garden is a mystery; perhaps it slithered down the roof. But there it was sure enough on the doorstep, and quite uninjured. It behaved in my bath in very much the same manner as another of its kind that was picked up uninjured on a Norfolk heath in December 1929. Both swam very high on the water and with a nautical roll, as it were, ill-balanced on a surface so unusually calm. Sometimes it vibrated its slightly open wings in a way that recalled the movements of a moth when expanding its wings after emergence from the chrysalis case, and not at all resembling the strong flaps that the bird gave to dry its pinions every now and then. Refreshed by a swim and a drink, it went off at great speed towards the coast when thrown into the air outside my house.

Ronald Garnett

Invading the woods

ℬ NOVEMBER 1943 ℭ

The war has invaded our woods. Carts and tractors, woodmen and land girls are busy among rides that echo with the 'din of hewing axes, crashing trees'. Only Scots pines are being felled at present. One is sorry to see the older and bigger trees go, but many of the younger ones, which form the greater proportion of those due to be cut down, can easily be spared. They grow far too thickly here, as do silver birches, the dead among which are at last being cleared away now that the need for logs to burn is so great.

As soon as they have been lopped, a tractor drags the larger pines to a ride and hauls them on to a lorry, which carries them away whole. The smaller ones are sawn where they fall into convenient lengths for pit props, piled into heaps according to their length and taken off on carts. Each onlooker finds pleasure in a different aspect of the scene – the hum of the circular saw, a sound as nostalgic as that of a threshing machine, a new view suddenly opening up before his eyes, or merely the sense of good work well done.

John Adams

Mangolds running short

DECEMBER 1943 Ꮽ

It is surprising how little the mention in war communiqués that 'bad weather conditions prevailed' conveys to one, but even at home, a waterlogged farm, blinding rain, sodden ground and animals to fodder is not amusing. Half a gale blowing during threshing, chaff cutting into your eyes and the wind snatching at the load on your pike, even if not accompanied by rain, can be very unpleasant. There is no time to wait for suitable weather; a shortage of threshing machines and worn ones breaking down all add to the smaller farmer's difficulties. They have now to cope with arable instead of only grassland. There is, too, the amount of stuff to store until transport and buyers can be found. All the good swedes in this part of the world have been sold for human consumption, and there seems likely to be a shortage of mangolds for feeding stock.

I am full of admiration for the older women – the over-50s and over-60s. They have proved astonishingly good workers. They have even taken their places at the threshing and have left the girls well behind. The best of our winter is that so often on the heels of a storm comes a mild springlike morning.

Gwen McBryde

Tits at the bottle

Ꮽ DECEMBER 1943 Ꮽ

One of my neighbours has been puzzled to know why each morning her bottle of Grade A milk should be found on her doorstep with the tinfoil cap torn open. The culprit was, of course, a tit, and it was caught red-handed one day last week by my daughter as she passed the house. Many accounts of this trick have been recorded from different parts of the country, but my neighbour has not heard of it. Now she takes care to see that her milk is quickly moved indoors. In this case it was the work of a blue tit. One of these used to come into my house through an open window and strip off the wallpaper, a most annoying habit and difficult to stop in summer.

Bullfinches have lately been coming to the garden, where I enjoy watching them at work among the honeysuckle fruits, to which they are welcome, but in spite of the fact that I have 'threaded' my forsythia bush, they vary their diet by stripping the buds from the longest shoots. The robins' song has dwindled almost to nothing and their song posts are seldom used, so checking up those carrying coloured rings has not proved as easy as I had hoped after the leaves had fallen. When pairing time comes round again, no doubt singing will increase, but my stock of coloured rings for newcomers is very small and cannot, I learn, be replenished until after the war is over.

Ronald Garnett

Wrens lend a hand

A week ago I wrote of my ill success in a search for waxwings in my own district. The following day, however, I was able through the kindness of a friend to watch a flock that it is generally agreed was in the neighbourhood of two hundred birds – an airborne invasion indeed! It was in a public park in a well-known seaside town that this exceptional flock had gathered, and when I heard of it, the birds had already been there for a week. An abundant supply of whitethorn berries provided their principal supply of food, but they varied their diet by taking a species of minute beetle that was rising from the ground to well over the tree tops. Some active young members of the WRNS captured a couple of specimens for me in no time and these have been identified by Manchester University Museum's coleopterist as belonging to one of some 800 species of the British *Staphylinidae*. From a bridge carrying the road over the glen it was possible to look down on the feeding birds from above, and many were the passersby who became bird-watchers, perhaps for the first time in their lives.

Ronald Garnett

The jumble war

℘ DECEMBER 1943 ☾

The war has caused one to clear out a great deal of junk, although much that is worn, patched or welded has been retained. I do not know if others suffer from the possession of some small object that has never been of the slightest use and yet defies destruction. For countless years, my desk has been haunted by a small, dried three-cornered fish. It was thrust upon me in my childhood by a native of Jamaica. I never wanted it and I don't want it now, but there it is. I dare say my old stud groom does not want the small crochet mat in green and black wool on his desk. It was my first handiwork done at an early age and there, I think, it ended. Once, in desperation, I posted a photograph from a table where I was writing. I didn't like to burn it. I do not remember how the recipient reacted.

Hard weather somewhere sent us the lapwings in quantity, and I am continually having to remove a robin from my hall, for fear the cats get him.

Gwen McBryde

BRAVE NEW WORLD

In the spring of 1944, a briskly intelligent writer from London, Mrs Robert Henrey, went on a tour by car along the Wye valley through Herefordshire, Monmouthshire and Gloucestershire and found the countryside in a sort of permanent doze. Five years of petrol shortages had retracted the locals' horizons, she decided. More than ever, they were like a neighbour of Gwen McBryde's in the hamlet of Kilpeck who never went beyond the boundaries of Herefordshire, and preferably no further than Leominster, because that was the only way to be a truly happy man. 'I even believe that some of the aged inhabitants were slipping back into their local jargon,' she wrote on her return to the capital, where she was shortly to publish *The Siege of London*, one of 30 books she wrote before her death at the age of 97, after slipping while feeding her hens in her own rural paradise in Normandy. 'If this state of affairs

193

went on long enough, who could tell but they would end by revert-
ing to the smock.'

But if a life of bicycles and Shanks's pony risked making some of
the older countryfolk sedentary and passive, there was an agent of
change in rural affairs which would soon wake them up. As never
before, the British countryside was playing host to thousands of new
arrivals, and unlike the tourists and weekenders of prewar days, they
were there to stay. The process began in late 1939, within a month
of the declaration of war on Germany on September 3, when thousands of children were evacuated from London and the major
regional cities in a programme based on the fear of apocalyptic
bombing. With hindsight we know that this was misplaced, for all
the devastation caused by the London and Coventry blitzes and the
later 'Baedeker raids' on cities, such as Exeter and Bath, that had
three stars in the German Baedeker guidebook. But the psychologi-
cal effect of the bombing of Guernica in the Spanish civil war had
been immense. As a highly critical report of the evacuation system
by the Fabian Society put it: 'The Ministry of Home Security was
obsessed by (HG) Wellsian visions of destruction.' Another critic
described the planners of the operation as exclusively 'military, male
and middle class'.

The result was notoriously problematic, with wailing children
(the sight of a cow was a terrifying novelty to many of them), desper-
ately anxious parents and impossible demands on rural authorities
such as Oxfordshire county council, which had to accept children
from more than 100 evacuating education authorities. Within less
than a year, nearly half the 734,883 unaccompanied children and
86% of the 260,276 who were evacuated with a parent or guardian
had returned home. However, that still left a lot. The way that many
of them took to rural life is fondly described from time to time in the
Country Diary, especially by Gwen McBryde, whose farm in south

Herefordshire was a haven for four years for dozens of city kids. She loved the way they saw the countryside, made imaginative suggestions and in several cases actually refused to go back home when the opportunity arose. For all the initial scares about vermin, disease and incomprehensible Cockney or Geordie, the close-knit world of Britain's villages benefited from this fresh blood.

Evacuees were not the only young arrivals. As the war's first harvest approached in the summer of 1940, the government revived the old Harvest Camps for Boys, which had struggled into life in the first world war, hampered by the lack of any budget to pay pocket money. Organisation was much better this time round, helped by the national sense in the early years of the war that Britain had her back to the wall and everyone needed to give a hand. Many schools cut holidays or tried to do away with them altogether, offering optional 'recreation' lessons, which included going out to the nearest farms to help. Much of the old rural calendar of children's farmwork set out in the 1867 Parliamentary Commission on the employment of women and children in agriculture survived, from coppicing in January to setting potatoes in April and the all-hands-on-deck climax of the August harvest. Roundhay high school in Leeds was typical in 'adopting' a farm at Minskip in North Yorkshire, after a neighbouring village turned a delegation of teachers away, suspicious that they wanted billets for yet more evacuees. The Roundhay students were paid the standard rate for unskilled farm labourers, giving the farmers a good deal because the teenagers worked with the vim of youth and the fun of tackling a novel task. Camps at Minskip were initially for three weeks but the farmer was so pleased that they were extended to eight. The boys had their breakfast before dawn, often hearing RAF bombers return to the big base at nearby Dishforth. They continued to camp annually until 1948, when the average of hours each boy worked weekly was a remarkable 41.09.

They had the opportunity for overtime because another tranche of new arrivals in the wartime countryside had mostly gone by 1948: the prisoners of war who agreed to work the land as an alternative to mouldering in guarded lines of huts. Most were Italian, who took a more relaxed approach to their supposed duty to escape than many of their German counterparts. Haymaking or harvesting mistletoe to the sound of opera arias on Gwen McBryde's farm was greatly preferable to trying to reach a Channel port in disguise through hostile territory. Even when the war was over and they were free to go, a substantial number who had no close relatives at home in Italy, and in a smaller number of cases Germany, opted to stay permanently. Most married locally and provided another source of new energy for the postwar countryside.

Much the best-known of the new arrivals, however, were the land girls, the smart and in most cases extraordinarily enthusiastic members of the Women's Land Army. As with the school harvest camps, the deployment of women in farming was far better organised than in the first world war. The volunteers themselves were also much more capable. There was still a social gulf between some of the billeted women and their hosts, notably in cases such as a young woman in Cambridgeshire who tried to bring her piano with her; but there was little criticism of the land girls' ability to work. Dressed in green jerseys, baggy brown breeches, brown felt slouch hats and khaki overcoats, they regularly adapted these in the summer, especially at harvest, with coloured blouses and frocks. Unlike their counterparts in 1914-18, they were in a world far removed from the Victorian countryside, where clergy such as the vicar of Ingoldthorpe had palpitations at the fact that 'the dress of farming women is almost of necessity immodest. When the crops are wet, they tuck their dresses between the legs often leaving their legs much exposed.' Heavy labouring was not their forte but there were subtler farming duties at which they excelled. More than 1,000 land girls worked as rat-catchers in Lincolnshire alone, two of them accounting for 12,000 of the vermin in one year, and that at the usually impressionable ages of 19 and 20. Tree-felling was another speciality, along with milking (which occupied almost a quarter of the WLA) and threshing. A former hairdresser struck a signal blow for equality by winning a ploughing competition in Yorkshire.

This cheerful bunch peaked in June 1944, the month of D-Day, when there were more than 80,000 at work – with several of them already drafting accounts of their experiences, whose titles alone tell the story. You can quickly track down *Pullet on the Midden* on the internet, Rachel Knappett's account of her time at Bath Farm in south-west Lancashire, where unusually she was the only land girl in a team of older, experienced and initially chauvinist men. She won them over, as did Shirley Joseph whose *If Their Mothers Only Knew* was published by Faber within a year of victory and is a cracking read. Land-girl enthusiasts may also want to try *Buttercup Gill, Cinderellas of the Soil, Dappled Sunlight, Lorna on the Land, In Baggy Brown Breeches and a Cowboy Hat, Victory Harvest, All in a Day's Work, Librarian on the Land* and perhaps the best of all in title terms, *Aw-arrh!*, an absorbing account of the wartime farming experiences of Ellen Mist.

The prisoners' eels

80 JANUARY 1944 03

The Italians who are doing some draining here have caught a lot of eels. The men stamp about in the mud in the ditch, and if an eel comes up, seize it and jerk it out on to the bank. They cook their catch for their dinner. Smoked eel is very good and eel in aspic is excellent. Today I had filleted pike; it is as good as trout and there was more of it. I must say it was much better than wartime sea-fish as it was so fresh.

I don't think I should like to make bread of home-ground wheat. I always wanted to grind grain between stones when I was a child and I don't think I ever managed it. It was never clear what a 'bolting sieve' or 'bolting clot' was like. They were terms in use in the 13th and 14th centuries. The finest bread made then was called 'simnel bread', the next quality 'wastel bread', probably from gateau, and the third quality was the 'puffe' or 'French bread' or 'cocklet'. These last were the farthing loaves, though prices varied at different periods. The lowest bread of all was mainly bran, or 'trete' as bran is still called in the north of England.

Gwen McBryde

Cowboy hat and baggy breeches, the uniform of the Women's Land Army

Visitors from the Fatherland

ഔ MARCH 1944 ର

A person living in East Prussia or Bohemia would have felt at home in one sense in an Oxford garden last week, for in it were seven or eight waxwings, which are one of the features of well-berried gardens in those districts in severe weather. 'Bohemian chatterers', their other familiar name, is less inappropriate than has been suggested, for it was their trilling, faint but distinctive, which I first mistook for that of some tit, that drew my attention to them. They were perched in a willow tree preening, but five or six soon flew away. These were very quick off the mark, flew high and fast, and looked very much like starlings. Their most noticeable feature as they swept past me was the yellow tip to their tails. The two that remained flew down to some hawthorns, where they could be watched at close range. The most obvious thing about them was their crests and black throats and, when I caught them side-face, their black and white wings. To get at the haws, they adopted the posture of a tit or a crossbill, and one momentarily hovered in front of a branch like a flycatcher or a willow wren.

John Adams

Hidden in the forest

ഔ MAY 2004 ର

Whether growing alongside a brook or clinging to air-vent walls in the underground passages at Uppark, ferns have their own special fascination. Many grow only in shade, but not so their brazen cousin, bracken. At this time of the year, it can be seen in many parts of the forest as a pale-green spring uncoiling from the turf. Later, it will become a waist-high, waving frond. In the late autumn, it will catch the sun and give a bronzed glow across the hillsides.

Though traditionally used by commoners for bedding and horticulture, bracken can be a problem. It is poisonous to ponies, highly invasive and eventually breaks down to a suffocating mulch, which chokes out smaller plants.

Final preparations are now under way to mark the 60th anniversary of the D-day landings. The forest was extensively used throughout the war, and strategically placed for an important role in the run-up to the invasion. It was home to many units waiting to cross the English Channel. Some of its great houses and estates became vital headquarters, and the forest lands themselves served as training grounds for all three services. Memorials to units stationed in the forest are to be found in a number of places. Those to the SOE at Beaulieu, and to the Canadian forces at Mogshade Hill, are of special interest.

During the D-Day preparations, it quickly became clear when the airfields were being established that there was going to be a battle with the bracken. I have been told that a specialist working party concluded that the only way to eliminate bracken was repeatedly to mow it, thereby weakening, and eventually killing, the rhizomes. Though laborious, this kept the airfields operational as long as needed.

But bracken is an important plant within the forest. Its shade benefits one of the forest's rarest plants, the wild gladiolus, and also provides shelter from the sun for cattle. It offers a safe haven in which does leave their fawns, and it is home to a vast array of insects, which are food for birds. Without it, the forest, and many of our landscapes, would be infinitely the poorer.

Rev Graham Long

The fields' changing face

Black-headed gulls are rapidly acquiring their chocolate-brown caps. Except for one, which, with complete disregard for fashion, had done this in mid-winter, I saw none with a complete cap till February 17; now there are many, and many more with half-brown hoods. Common gulls, too, which will soon be on their way north, have lost most of their dingy head feathers, which in some cases are already quite white.

Tree sparrows continue to interest us. A pair has occupied a box on a bird table, and there they stood side by side caressing one another with their bills – an act of courtship I had not known them perform before. One of another pair struggled with a feather into a second box while its mate, with masterly inactivity, perched on top and watched.

The face of the countryside continues to change. I took a count of more than 200 fields and found that only 24% were permanent pastures and the rest arable – very different from the old days, when so much of the land was devoted to stock-raising. And almost all the old tall thorn fences have gone, some of them cut down to the ground to let sun and air have access to the ploughland.

Arnold Boyd

Plea for the rooks

The determined effort of War Agricultural Committees to reduce the number of rooks has been called in question in more than one quarter. My farmer friends all look on rooks with favour; such grain as the birds take is limited in quantity and they feel sure that this is more than balanced by the destruction of wireworms and leatherjackets. Considering that the Agricultural Research Council has sponsored an inquiry into the status and feeding habits of the rook and that in one Cheshire district at least numbers are down by one third, the birds should surely be left in peace for the present. Rooks are long-lived; one, which was an adult when I ringed it in July 1933, was recently shot at the nest a mile-and-a-half away – at least 12 years old.

On May Day, a black tern, which a friend had already seen earlier in the day, was hawking flies over the mere; it flew at a much greater height than usual, as if insects had risen high in the air; but it made an occasional headlong but graceful fall to water level as it beat up against the wind. Cormorants are on the move – I saw eight on a raft on the mere today – and I am told that Greenland wheatears have been seen. A careful moorhen in my field has built an open nest in the rushes but keeps her eggs partly covered with leaves.

Arnold Boyd

The engineers' base

ॐ JANUARY 2007 ॐ

In the first feeble light of a winter dawn, I often find solitude among the woods of Sandy Warren. Today the air is dank and still, and as I pause at the top of the bridlepath, looking down the sunken track towards the common, there is silence but for the faint patter of water dripping from the trees. I start my descent, and almost at once a robin sets up a thin, high call of alarm, reminding me that I am not truly alone. Somewhere nearby, a crow rising from its roost gives a single harsh caw of alarm. When I followed this path in the autumn, crisp leaves chased round my feet in the wind. Now brown masses of soggy dead vegetation lie plastered over the banks.

As the path broadens and grows steeper under tall pines towards the bottom, the open heath beckons to the left, but my eyes are drawn down to the honey, grey and tawny lumps of brick rubble embedded in the sand path. The heavy autumn rains have washed the silt out from around some of these bricks, so that in places the path begins to resemble a cobbled street. Brick debris lines all of the tracks around these heaths and woods, a poignant reminder of desperate times. In 1944, troops of the Royal Engineers were posted here to practise for D-Day landings on the beaches of Normandy. Their heavy amphibious vehicles would have gouged deep channels in the soft sand, so rubble from the bombed Victorian terraces of London's East End was sent to lay a Cockney foundation on these rural tracks.

A generation after the war ended, an estate sprung up on the north side of Sandy to house 'the London overspill'. Perhaps some of the local people who walk this bridlepath may be stepping on the homes of their ancestors.

Derek Niemann

D-Day Diaries

ဢ JUNE 1994 শ্ব

In 1932 I gave my brother, two years my senior, *The Ornithologists' Field Book*. The preliminary list of British birds was duly ticked off as his records increased, but the main part of the book, lined blank pages, was untouched for the following 12 years. Ian, a telegraphist, had joined the London Fire Service at the outbreak of war, but getting bored during the period before the blitz, managed to resign and join the RAF. From then on his lips were sealed; we assumed that he was connected with a hush-hush service involving usually air force uniforms but sometimes khaki with an anchor emblem on the shoulder – hints of what we came to know as Combined Ops. I took possession of his bird diary after his death a few years ago, and found that he had written it up almost daily since his arrival in Normandy on June 7. The entries were terse, such as 'good dry landing – shot at by E-boat on way, and a sniper on landing. Bout of digging our lovely dugout. Noisy night.' But in the early days there was no mention of birds and it was only in later conversations I learned that he had flushed a peregrine on the final ascent of the cliff, and though tempted to look for the nest, continued his hurried upward journey. No hints as to the activities of his group, but when he was demobbed all came out – his was a very secret unit with a waggon containing the newly invented radar apparatus. He loved telling of how they were instructed to let no one in, not even the C-in-C, without written authorisation. Later Ian seemed to pay greater attention to birds, and was very impressed by a noisy night of Manx shearwater calls, with which he had become familiar on a joint visit to the Pembroke island of Skokholm. There were references to passages of migrants such as yellow wagtails, wheatears, and redstarts. Ian returned home unscathed except for a broken wrist from a champagne-induced tumble from a lorry. His next bird note of interest was of black redstarts nesting high up on Paddington Station.

Bill Campbell

Moths in the blackout

❧ June 1944 ☙

A disused town dump at Northwich, now covered with vegetation, has produced this year a wonderful crop of the fungus known as the shaggy ink cap (*Coprinus comatus*). It is a tall, long, pale fungus with yellow patches, and like many other forms of life, including the human, it is infinitely more attractive in its appearance when it is young. It is said to be edible, but later its gills turn black and it deteriorates into an object of forbidding aspect; it is little wonder that it is never even considered as a possible food by the great majority, who enjoy and even pay large sums for the common mushroom.

Owing to the blackout, few moths come indoors nowadays, but a white tip clothes moth (*Trichophaga tapetzella*) flew in and settled on a wall. White-headed and with dark and whitish oddly shaped wings, which rise in a peak over its body, it would escape notice in the open, so strongly does it resemble a bird dropping. Its larvae feeds on such things as rugs and skins, and I remember a big brood that emerged from an old forgotten horse cloth thrown carelessly into a shippon corner. Fortunately it does not seem to be common in Cheshire, where it has been recorded from only two or three places.

Arnold Boyd

Victory through herbs
෨ JULY 1944 ඈ

The old man paused by the yarrow to say, 'The finest herb that grows!' The Greeks knew the healing powers of *Achillea millefolium*, and it is valued by our folk, who call it 'thousandleaf' from the minutely cut feathery foliage. Its flowerheads bloom daintily, as a good example will show. Tight clustered buds open pin-points of white, furled rays which turn into cones that flatten to reveal disc florets, with their anthers bright gold at first. A few heads, however, are pink-tinged, others the rose of cultivated milfoil. Though dried as a brew for feverish colds, yarrow's use in salves seems to be obsolete.

Garden herbs need watching now. Harvested before flowering, when scent and leaf-texture are just right, their drying and storage are a pleasure. 'Digging for Victory' has encouraged interest in sweet pot-herbs with their musical names and individual savours, which link today with the middle ages, when herb gardens provided plants to improve food, to prevent disease (in theory at least), and to sweeten the carpet of rushes. Clumps of chives are a proof of this interest, for a few years ago many of the growers had never seen this herb.

Ambrose Heath

London can take it

🔊 JULY 1944 ༼

Travelling south from Yorkshire in the middle of the month, it was remarkable to watch the harvest ripening, as it were under one's very eyes. In Yorkshire hay harvest was in full swing and the wheat still green, but as one passed from county to county, the wheat became more and more golden, and later field after field was seen patterned with stooks. After several days in a built-up area, it was refreshing to spend a few hours beside the river on a Sunday afternoon, watching these marvellous people of the London region boating, bathing and enjoying the sun as though flying bombs did not exist and their homes were safe from wanton destruction. Nothing can shake them.

In a flooded sandpit by the river, a great crested grebe, still in summer plumage, turned on its side to preen its snow-white underparts, and while we sat at tea in a suburban garden the song of a coal tit came from the only fir tree to be seen, and from it a barred woodpecker flew off on a graceful, curving line of flight.

Ronald Garnett

While the cat's away

&c) AUGUST 1944 &c

There has been no preservation of game for five years, no bracken
has been cut for bedding, no hedges have been dressed, no thinning
of coverts has been attempted – the fellside, long a sanctuary for
feathered and ground vermin, has gone wilder even than during the
last war. Magpies, jays, carrion crow, rooks and buzzards have taken
complete possession of this foothill, with its peeps through the trees
of the far-off mountain ranges. Foxes abound – the huntsman says
there are enough here to keep a pack going the whole of a season;
badgers from a nearby colony have set up new quarters among the
gorse and broom; stoat and weasel overrun the ground. The ground
vermin are seldom seen – the bracken conceals their movements –
but there is much evidence of the ill they do. The badgers give themselves away by the litter they leave after tearing out the hives of wild
bees. Small birds are nearly all gone. Sparrowhawk and kestrel drive
away winchat, thrush, blackbird and robin. But there remains a cage
of wire-netting, 10 feet square and six feet in height, which has with-
stood the storms, and through the hole in its roof descend carrion
crow and magpie, and on one occasion a buzzard, to feast on the
carrion put on the ground as bait. The jay alone resists temptation.
Not one of his kind has been trapped.

George Muller

A curious object

&c) AUGUST 1944 &c

The dreary July has produced a great spate of weeds; labour is
scarce and gardens and hedgerows are smothered with heavy loads

of nettles, goosegrass and giant convolvulus. Paratroops have been launched in millions, and the airborne species have assured their perpetuity.

Recently, I went to see some friends who live in a village in the Low Country. It is a secluded little place, distinguished by an old Norman church and some fine oak trees, with the green grass growing all around; no gas, no electricity, and even the water has to be brought from the spring. However, with the aid of wireless and one bus a week, they keep themselves in touch with the 20th century. In September 1939, two monuments appeared, one at each end of the village street. They were erected by the Air Raid Precautions and labelled 'gas detector'. These objects have been regarded with the greatest respect by the villagers, which is rather surprising, seeing that any easily removable timber is likely to vanish. Nature, however, has been at work on the boards; one is almost buried in a grove of nettles and the other has been converted into an object of real beauty by the great bindweed. My friends told me that they had recently installed a new vicar and he had to mow himself in.

Ronald Garnett

Schoolboy harvesters

ஐ AUGUST 1944 ௬

However long a drought may last, there would always be the race against time when harvesters work until late at night to get in the grain before the ominous clouds burst. A fitful wind will blow from south and west, turning up branches so that the pale undersides of leaves show; and the woodpecker calls as he shoots by. In the morning, the labourers return looking tanned and tired. Clearing up rain-sodden gear and surveying drooping sheaves is a cheerless

Schoolboys bring in a bumper harvest in 1945

occupation. But against this are the ranks of trim sacks of grain in safety in the barn.

Schoolboys from the camps have been in request and seem to enjoy themselves in spite of such things as water shortage and various little difficulties – an identity card hidden beneath a rick, and so on. Apples are forward, and so thick on some trees that they have to be gathered to prevent the trees from breaking down. Last year some young trees of strawberry norman were so heavily laden that they split right in half. They had not been pruned since the first year of the war or possibly this might not have happened.

Gwen McBryde

Caterpillars and the blitz

✆ SEPTEMBER 1944 ✆

The elephant hawk moth, as I have mentioned on several occasions, is now to be found frequently in this part of England, where before the spread of its main food plant, the rosebay willowherb, it was far from common. The latest and most remarkable instance of this widespread dispersal is reported by a friend who found a caterpillar feeding in the centre of Manchester, at the corner of Corporation Street and Hodson's Court. The windborne seeds of the plant may be seen travelling across country and town, and bombed areas have been specially favoured, but it is less easy to understand how this moth came to lay its eggs in the centre of the city and to find the proper food plants on a comparatively small blitzed oasis of weeds in a great desert of roofs and streets, strong flyer though it be.

Arnold Boyd

The Romeos clock off

ᔕ OCTOBER 1944 ᘗ

I was out at dusk to seek help for the threshing; Italians having proved more trouble than they were worth, arriving late and leaving soon after four o'clock tea, our men said they would do without 'the Romeos'. On my round I went to see how many of our old cider trees would have to be replaced. There are many with huge limbs broken off. There were big chunks of mistletoe on the fallen branches, which no doubt had helped in the destruction. I looked up and saw some swans flying over from the direction of the Monnow, winging their flight to a lake near the timber line. I passed by the big badger earth on my way home; there is much going on there; a great deal of earth has recently been thrown up, and stout footprints show clearly on the soil.

Our newly planted fields are already pricked out in hues of green, and we await our chance of getting the sugar beet, which has done well. Marigolds have been damaged by rabbits but are otherwise good. There are still raspberries and a certain amount of Alpine strawberries in my garden. Let us hope we may get an Indian summer.

Gwen McBryde

No fishing; more gulls

ᔕ DECEMBER 1944 ᘗ

The curtailment of fishing operations in earlier winters of the war has brought about an increase in the number of great black-backed gulls inland, and it is not surprising that the occasional glaucous gulls, which visit the east coast in winter, should sometimes follow them. An immature bird of this species was found on the flooded marshes on December 5, when again the number of species of ducks was eight, a fine drake pintail having joined the general assembly. But yesterday we found that much of the water had drained back into the river whence it had come, ice covered much of what remained, and the ducks were standing in groups upon the ice, though many had gone elsewhere. The vast masses of lapwings that had been seen 10 days before, resting idly at the waterside during the period of full moon, were now scattered widely and were feeding with golden plover on many cultivated fields. While we stood watching the ducks, a commotion occurred, first among some distant lapwings and then among the ducks, as a peregrine arrived. After perching a moment in a tall tree, it circled round us on winnowing wings to disappear again further upstream.

Ronald Garnett

Keeping up the paths

℘ DECEMBER 1944 ℘

The disuse of rural footpaths is a matter of some concern to lovers of the country; and there is a society that does noble work in maintaining these rights of way, but we must remember that many are used nowadays by 'ramblers' from the cities and not by the farmer and cottager by whom they were originally established. Bicycles have done more to close footpaths ('padways', the old Cheshire folk call them) than all the landlords in England. 'Jog on, jog on the footpath way' no longer appeals to the labourer, who finds a quicker though longer way by the high road. Ploughing up and diversion of paths have reasonably been allowed during the war, but the villager will do little, I fear, to reopen rights of way he seldom or never uses.

Rural parish councils are not really interested; a request to replace a broken bridge was met with the original and brilliant reply:

'There's a war on'! A farmer recently told me that I was now the only person to use a path across his fields. Rights of way have no enemy so powerful as local apathy.

Arnold Boyd

Birds on the advance through Europe

℘ DECEMBER 1944 ℘

Song thrushes began their late autumn song on November 19 and sang regularly every day till about December 4, since when I have heard none. November song varies greatly in volume from year to year; it was shown in the Bird Song Inquiry that thrushes were apt to stop singing at the end of the month or early in December, and this is what they have done this season. We may expect song again about Christmas time unless the weather is very cold, but really severe weather checks, and often completely stops, the thrushes' song.

A letter from a friend in the army tells of the birds of Belgium and Holland: a sandpiper in an anti-tank ditch; black redstarts under the stands of a former football ground and about the ruins of a Dutch church; six cranes flying over Hertogenbosch; crested tits and firecrests in a wood; and tree sparrows in a derelict farm north of Nijmegen, at Elst. Black redstarts like ruined buildings for their nests, as bombed London has shown, and as the supply of suitable nesting sites to a great extent regulates the number of birds in any area, they at least may profit by the laying waste of unfortunate Belgian and Dutch homes.

Arnold Boyd

Who needs to buy toys?

℘ DECEMBER 1944 ℘

The shortage of toys is, I believe, more of a disappointment to the grown-ups who cannot buy them than to the children, who seem to have regained the almost lost art of amusing themselves with pretences and making toys for themselves. These toys often show much ingenuity.

I remember with respect the concoctions of my sisters – shoe-boxes covered with the famous 'turkey red' of that era. The lid was placed upright at the end of the box, forming the 'tester', and curtains of spotted muslin were attached. Patchwork quilts were made of bits of satin and brocade gleaned from the ragbag. When the beds were complete they served for our pet kittens, who willingly lay on their backs with paws out on the lace-edged sheet. As for dolls, all the 'best dolls' were only to be played with on Christmas afternoon and some other special occasions. They had served several generations of children. There was the wax baby doll with real eyelashes and hair and lovely long robes. And the Parisian dolls sent by a lady from St Petersburg complete with pale blue trunk and trays filled with exquisitely made outfits, including the finest Shetland shawls for going out to parties. The dolls were called Arnia and Gonlia.

When Mrs Anna Lea Merritt, the American artist, painted a portrait of the little girls, they got her to paint a picture of their dolls as well. She told me that in her picture *Love and Life*, now in the Tate Gallery, she had copied the head from the portrait of the youngest little girl and put it in her picture.

Gwen McBryde

CHAPTER TEN

TERRIBLE ECHOES

As the end of the war at last approached, a family in the Peak District village of Chinley received a letter from their son, Major Rodney Gee, which was full of the hope that the weary people of Britain were at last allowing themselves to feel. His address was not a coveted one; the prison camp of Oflag 1X in Hesse, but he was beginning to sense that the keys would soon turn and allow him to go home. 'The crocuses are at last in full bloom here,' he wrote. 'Swallows came on Easter Sunday – we have a huge and beautiful lot of birds and they are fed from nearly every window.' The next day he went on a picnic and dug up some ferns and foxgloves, which he planned to take after liberation to replant in the family's garden in Derbyshire.

The optimism was widely shared, as the British countryside too began to take stock of the changes brought by war and the best way to adapt them to the future. The false start of Lloyd George's 'Land fit for heroes' after the first world war had rooted itself in the national psyche. There was a determination that equivalent maps of a new Jerusalem, such as Sir William Beveridge's welfare and social security proposals and the germ of ideas that would become the National Health Service, should be effective and a success.

Rooted in the past for decades, the shires had been transformed by the mechanisation of agriculture and the influx of new workers; the platoons of evacuees, prisoners-of-war and land girls were joined in the final years of the conflict by allied and Commonwealth troops from all over the world. Wartime dispensed with old suspicions and dislike of 'comers-in'; there was a response in most rural areas to a national appeal from army welfare officers for a particular welcome to be given to Indian and African soldiers who might find their new surroundings strange and British reserve as chilly as the weather. 'Unparalleled numbers of troops are quartered in every part of the country,' said the appeal, whose main concern was that Dominion forces should not feel snubbed. 'It is immensely worthwhile for everyone to ask himself how he can entertain a few of these splendid fellows in however small a way – if only to a smoke, a drink or a talk.' United States troops were reckoned to be able to look after themselves on the whole, but guidance notes advised villagers not to be put out if some of the GIs complained about the absence of that great American institution, the country club.

Victory in Europe in May 1945 and over Japan three months later brought relief and a brief pause in the general feeling that the new battle, to win the peace and build a better Britain, had to get under way. Trestle tables and bunting were brought out everywhere, and children were given souvenir mugs while their parents received an illuminated celebration address from King George VI. In some parts of the country, a red apple and a packet of dried egg powder was added to the children's package: a gift from the people of Canada, as the slightly mystified recipients were told. Church bells rang again and, most spectacularly of all, everywhere blackout curtains were taken down and lights blazed.

Once again, as after the first world war, planning was set in hand for commemoration; names were added to the war memorials that had become such a feature of country communities in the 1920s. There was an even greater emphasis on finding socially useful ways of honouring the dead, through pavilions, scholarships, village halls and playing fields. People did not talk superficially about a 'war to end wars', but there was an unspoken feeling that this time, the settlement with the defeated must get things right. The emphasis was on rebuilding a new and solidly democratic Germany, Japan and Italy. The United Nations' Charter was signed within a year of VE Day at San Francisco in the United States, which had helped to lame the UN's weak predecessor, the League of Nations, by refusing to join it or to ratify its peace-keeping covenant.

The heady time was not to last for long. The Soviet Union's iron curtain descended, creating cold war tensions, which were to last for almost 50 years, and the United States' equally steely refusal to bail out Britain's battered economy was devastating. In both world wars, bread rationing was avoided in Britain. Now, between June 1946 and July 1948, it was introduced. Warfare also returned. British troops were in action in Greece, Palestine, Malaya and on a scale reminiscent of the world wars, in Korea. The second half of the 20th century was to see increasing prosperity and a transformation in society that has been especially marked in the British countryside, almost entirely for the better. But it is not possible to draw a line under any entry in the *Manchester Guardian's* Country Diary since 1945 and say: 'That is it. That is where Wartime Country Diaries end.' Terrible echoes of the 20th century's two great conflicts persist, as more names are added to village war memorials and parish churches hold funerals for young men who did not come home safely from Afghanistan and Iraq. The final words of the final diary in this collection, by Paul Evans, are sobering.

Homes for heroines

ଶ୍ଦ JANUARY 1945 ଔ

Rural housing is an important facet of the many-sided national problem of agriculture, and talk of plans and materials, of laid-on services and gadgets is common, and not least among the young women who, as members of the Land Army, came to the countryside, stuck to the work, liked it, and elected to stay on the land when peace returns. A girl fresh from office work and city life used to say, as she knitted in the firelight after a hard day on the tractor, that she would never go back to the town. Just before Christmas there came a sample of her bridescake, for she is now happy as a farmer's wife.

The housing question recalls an old cottage not long ago destroyed in the course of road improvements. It built on the 'cruck' system of naturally bent oak timber fixed together by a ridgebeam, thus forming a cage on which roof-timbers were laid to be covered with thatch, the spaces between the side supports being filled with panels of wattle and daub. Such a building could be extended quite easily by lean-to additions, and even today quite a number of such cottages survive. We watched the demolition all afternoon while the workmen with their expert means of destruction toiled and tussled to pull apart the 'cruck' at one end of this little house, probably of Tudor date, whose stoutness, a testimonial to its long-gone builders, surprised everybody. Game to the end, it was at last laid low.

Ambrose Heath

The tourists return

'May I speak to the master of the house?' A woman's voice came over the 'phone. 'I'm t'maister of t'hoose.' The tone was grim, suggesting that the mistress was proprietress and 't'maister' of any menfolk around. Then: 'What d'ye want?' 'Rooms.' 'Loavin days, ye're early. When does tha want them for?' 'Easter.' Some moments of silence followed. Evidently 't'maister' was thinking things over. The talk went on.

'Ah cuddent think on it. Ah divvent think Ah'll have any visitors this year. It's fair horse-wark takking people in when ye've neah maids. Ah only had yan last summer and she left early. Visitors hed to dubbin theer own shoes and their women-folk hed to mak t'beds. It'll be the seame this time if we hev visitors at aw. Dost tha want to coom thissel?' 'No.' 'What's thoo askin for then?' 'Oh, just friends.' 'Well, I've telt tha. Mind, we cud full t'pleace, if Ah cud git help, right to t'end of October.'

The receiver was about to be replaced when the voice came again. 'Where's thoo speakin from?' An industrial town was named. 'Any lassies theer?' 'Lots of them.' 'What're they doing?' 'All sorts of things.' 'What swort of lasses be they?' 'Great big strapping lasses.' 'Golly, send us sum alang.'

George Muller

Easter on the farm

The countryside is decking itself out for Easter. The pale green of the willows and the opening buds of the blackthorn give a dainty air to the thickets. I have been watching a yellow-haired girl with sheep bobbing along at her heels, a collie circling round. They are through the gate, the girl lifts her hand, the little sheepdog stops dead, the girl skips into a tractor that has its engine running, and drives off down the grass in the dingle among daffodils and by a bank where blue and white violets are flowering. Then over the stream and into a field that has just been sown.

An Italian attaches the seed drill to the tractor and off they go to another field. The clang of a roller can be heard where an oat field is being rolled and the hum of the caterpillar tractor as it ploughs. You can hear too that delightful, spring-like sound, the soft laughing low note of the green woodpecker.

I have been cutting out the dead wood from a patch of roses, mostly York and Lancasters, and some damask, moss and dwarf roses, but some seem to have become climbers. I came upon four of last year's nests like saucers of wiry grass loosely made.

Gwen McBryde

The banality of tractors

ᑭ MAY 1940 ᑫ

I am told that stone fruit has been spoilt by frost, but up here I cannot see that it is damaged. I have lost my strawberry crop – some late blooms may open but the advanced fruit is blackened. Below in the valley, oaks look singed and shrivelled and early potatoes are cut down. I suppose there will be some more apple blossom but the trees look brown now.

The scarcity of plover nowadays is a serious matter. They were great scavengers of wireworm. People collecting the eggs for sale have left us with hardly a plover. Wireworm seems to come to the surface when the sun has warmed the ground and to go down again if it is cold or wet. In the middle of the day, when it is sunny, I have seen rooks digging for them.

Old days on farms used to be very pleasant, with workers personally interested in the stock and proud of their teams. There is nothing to be proud of about tractors, even when they do consent to work. I sometimes think of an admirable cowman who said his father had 'a sweet life as he had never been beyond Hereford and Leominster'.

Gwen McBryde

Counting the rooks

℘ MAY 1945 ℘

The laborious but interesting job of making a census of rooks' nests, which has occupied many observers this spring, has been made more difficult by the early leaves on many of the nesting-trees. Some of the more active observers have suffered (with apologies to Mr Ben Travers) from acute attacks of 'rookery neck'. An area of 64 square miles in which I counted 1,434 nests in 1931 held 1,005 last year and only 942 this year, a reduction from about 23 to the square mile to under 15. Although the majority are in sycamore, beech, elm, oak and ash, the most prevalent large trees, I have found many nests in Scotch pine, alder and poplar, some in cherry, birch, larch, hawthorn and other trees, and one where the boughs of an elder and an oak had intertwined. In 1939 I had three groups under observation in Lombardy poplars, in which the birds must have difficulty in finding a purchase for their nests.

There has been a breaking up of some old colonies due to felling and other disturbances, and on several large estates the nests are now distributed in smaller and more scattered colonies. Those rooks known locally as 'Lord Barrymore's pigeons' had to find new lodgings when the big beeches at Marbury Hall gates, near Northwich, were felled and the estate passed to others; those known with similar bucolic humour as 'Lord Crewe's canaries' have left their big rookery at Crewe Hall, where, so I am told, they used to be left undisturbed by their old landlord before this estate too changed hands. The break-up of large estates makes all the more necessary the creation of nature reserves.

Arnold Boyd

Jabber, babble and discord

ℰꙮ June 1945 ꙮℛ

In 1938, when a survey of the British black-headed gull colonies was made, we knew of three gulleries in Cheshire, but it now appears that there was probably a fourth in existence at that time, on the border of Cheshire and Lancashire. In 1928, so I am told, a few gulls first nested on a great stretch of mud and long grass by the Ship canal in the Mersey valley, 13 miles north of the ancient gullery in Delamere forest, where they are known to have nested as long ago as 1617. They have bred only intermittently since they occupied the new site, but this season there are more than ever before – 200 to 300 pairs was our estimate.

Under a tree in a little mereside wood, I found a beautiful carpet moth (*Mesoleuca albicillata*), one I have not seen there before and one not common in Cheshire. Its English name describes it well; its white wings are marked with dark patches and grey lines so situated that when the moth rests on a tree trunk, an irregular white patch is all that can be seen, and it looks at a distance like a scrap of paper left on a nail when a notice has been pulled down. This wood is full of 'jabber, babble and discord' (to quote from one of Mr Churchill's vivid speeches), for a pair of carrion crows and a pair of kestrels that have nested there evidently distrust one another utterly.

Arnold Boyd

The war's legacy

ஐ AUGUST 1945 ை

Those who are interested in the prosperity of the land, whether from utilitarian or sentimental motives does not matter much, have been greatly concerned during the past few years at the legacy that will be left behind through the wartime shortage of agricultural labour. The immediate concern, of course, is the difficulty experienced in finding the hands 'to plough and sow, to reap and mow' in order to secure

Bombsites rich in wildflowers scarred London for 30 years after the second world war

the nation's food supply, at least until it can be augmented by imports. But what of the aftermath? A day or two ago I was wandering along a country lane thinking: 'How long will it take to clear up the mess?' Both sides of the lane were cluttered up with spear thistle, and years of jack labour had allowed them to spread over the fields as far as the eye could reach. Some had already shed their seeds, and the area around was thickly carpeted with their light, downy, white parachutes. On an average-sized plant I counted 141 heads. I selected one, nearly ripe, took it home and dissected it, and found it contained 287 parachutes, at the base of each of which was a seed. It is true that nature is very prodigal in seed production, and that the big majority of the thistle seeds are among nature's casualties; nevertheless, the remainder will form the nucleus of a packet of trouble for the farmers of the immediate future.

John Harrison

Soggy Italians

ဆာ SEPTEMBER 1945 ရ

According to the newspapers, there are parts of England where the weather has been better than here. We have now had eight days of rain. In the Monmouth country there are acres of corn out and barley that can be cut by no sort of machine. Extra labour now consists of a few unwilling Italians who are all against getting their boots wet. They chat of wine and soap, cider, sandwiches and cigarettes. I still have one field of barley uncut, but it is short-strawed and has not gone down. A farmer told me he had to cut the bottom off the corn sheaves as clover had grown up into them.

Cider fruit has come on suddenly and all but the late perry pears are ready. Sheep sales have begun. The Clun forest breed are rapidly gaining in popularity; there were buyers from as far apart as Northumberland and Hampshire. A man who does hedging here said he had sold six tonnes of damsons last week. He has a small place on a steep hillside that appears to need very little attention. He plants a few young damsons each year that have seeded themselves in his garden.

Gwen McBryde

The value of berries

ℬ SEPTEMBER 1945 ℭ

The berry harvest has ripened all too soon. In six weeks, the redwings will be arriving on this coast hungry and seeking the rowan trees normally carrying an abundant store of food so temptingly displayed. But already the mistle-thrushes are at work, and these, with the resident finches, will soon strip the scarlet bunches, scattering what they do not eat. Elderberries too are turning black, and those that overhang our garden wall will be turned into puddings and pies long before the starling hordes arrive from overseas. It was wartime scarcity that made us realise how good these berries are, rivalling blackberries and much more easily acquired. Robins are reappearing in numbers all over the village. Some are singing, but their ticking cries are more frequently heard just now. Two, which came exploring in the garden, were strangers, for they carried no coloured rings; a fresh supply of these is now available. A third that appeared one day had lost an eye and would soon be caught by one of the many cats which prowl around.

Ronald Garnett

Moulded by war

ɮ NOVEMBER 2005 ʗ

The frost that has scarcely lifted for days has given the fallen leaves an early crispness. Up to midday cold mistiness shrouds the tree-tops. Spiders' webs, to my grandson, look spun with chewing gum. The edges of smaller lakes are frozen.

By noon the sun is breaking through, casting long shadows among the trees. It lights up the shimmering surface of Dockens Water to reveal the transformation that is taking place. The water rises across the forest at Fritham and works its way south-west to enter the Hampshire Avon near Ringwood. Its course was greatly modified by work to drain wetlands, for grazing and plantations, in the 19th and early 20th centuries. But the impact was minor compared to the second world war, when demand for sand and gravel became paramount – the Avon valley has rich deposits that have been used since Roman times.

In past months, the Hampshire and Isle of Wight Wildlife Trust, supported by other agencies, has restored two small lengths of the water to their original course. There is now breadth and a meandering flow, and with the clearance of the over-shaded banks, the way has been prepared for a much more diverse habitat. It is hoped that sea trout will once again spawn and that other species will return.

This afternoon, though, the sun sparkles on the rippling water, giving the amber shingle bed a warming glow. Rose hips and unripened blackberries add colour to the track alongside. The official pamphlet speaks of a river reborn. To me the scene has the delight of a prisoner whose life sentence has been quashed and says now I can live.

Graham Long

Remembering S for Sugar

Like iron filings charged with magnetic energy, figures on the skyline cannoned into each other or flew apart. Why we behaved in so extraordinary a fashion was nothing to do with Faraday's laws, owing more to 75mph gales streaming across the serried ridges of the Coniston fells. Quirky gusts would randomly select one of us and frog-march them forward. Anyone who happened to be in the way would be blissfully unaware of the impending collision as, mountain jacket hood pulled down over their head, they tried to keep their feet away from the huge drop down crags into the cove below. Were it not for the express purpose of this gathering, there would have been a unanimous exodus back to the cars parked on Wrynose Pass before any further height had been reached. Instead, the wind and rain only served as a timely reminder that in similar conditions Halifax bomber 'S for Sugar' crashed into the fellside just below the summit of Great Carrs in 1944. Hence the gathering as we continued up into the mist on Armistice Day two weeks ago. Once we had reached the Lake District's most visited aircraft crash site, marked by a large piece of undercarriage still embedded in the rocks, we collected around the vicar of Coniston. His dedication of a plaque to the brave young aircrew who had died was poignant; the sounds of the Last Post from a drenched bugler were torn away in the gale. Three air force officers in best-blue uniforms took the salute, incongruous among a throng of people clad in Gore-Tex and streaming with rain-drops. Beyond the be-poppied wooden cross jammed in the cairn, should have been ethereal views of Scafell. Instead, a wall of cloud met the eye. And so the descent began back down the ridge, with slippery rocks being obstacles to avoid as the wind increased its fury.

As a mountain rescue team member said; 'It is as well the occasion was not made public.'

Tony Greenbank

A mighty memorial

ℰ℧ NOVEMBER 2005 ℃ℛ

We climbed by way of wet nettles up the north-east flank of High Wheeldon under a grey blanket of cloud that spat down unfriendly showers. Then we came to the 422m (1,384ft) summit of this 'wheel hill' – a stone circle or some unrecorded mill in the valley below? As early as 1251, it was called Wildon, but no one has come up with a certain explanation for the name.

Upon the grassy cone, a commemorative plaque announces that the mayor of Buxton gave the hilltop to the National Trust in 1946, to the memory of the people of Derbyshire and Staffordshire killed in the second world war. There is no finer view of hill and dale in all the White Peak of this National Park. Even on this day of fitful drizzle we could pick out the sharp-profiled reef knolls of Chrome Hill and Parkhouse Hill to the north and across the green-dale bottom of the upper Dove, to the tree-topped ridge behind which Longnor was lurking. It was a prospect of flat lighting that demanded a shaft of sunlight to punctuate some flank or other. None came. As we traversed the dale's floor, passing into Staffordshire, we negotiated boot-sucking marsh and tracks now running with water.

Heavy rain set in. The deluge continued on and off until dusk and we squelched our way to Fawside Edge. Another traverse of ill-drained pasture below Hollinsclough moor delivered us to the bridle-way down to Hollinsclough hamlet, a rock staircase no motor vehicle could negotiate, eroded to a stony ravine flushed by drainwater.

Roger Redfern

Pillbox in the brambles

℘ SEPTEMBER 2001 ℘

A flicker of movement amongst the impenetrable tangle of black-thorn smothering the second world war concrete anti-tank defences turned out to be a young stonechat. A little further away, another perched on a long bramble stem, buffeted by the early autumn gale. Broken white clouds raced overhead and the wind whipped spray off the wave crests, but here, in the hollow of the dunes, the orange diadem spider that had woven its orb web amongst the ripening blackberries hung motionless in the middle of its snare.

In the dune slacks where rabbits had close-grazed the turf, the last of the summer flowers – fell wort, viper's bugloss, thyme, lady's bedstraw and hawkweeds – were running to seed, and the white bryony trailing through the brambles glistened with scarlet berries. Along the footpath, we stopped every few yards to admire a sunbather: first, two basking common hawker dragonflies, wings pressed close to the warm sand, then grasshoppers chirruping from their perches on broken seashells. Once we disturbed a young lizard, soaking up the sun amongst the withered grasses, and watched it wriggling away until it disappeared into the tangle of roots.

We climbed to the top of the highest dune. An undulating, waving sea of lyme and marram grass stretched along the dune tops. Not a single living soul on the beach, where pools left by the receding tide glittered in the sunshine. A few swallows hawked for flies and, out at sea, terns plunge-dived for fish. Still further out, towards Coquet Island, I could just make out gannets fishing their way down the coast, plummeting into the waves.

Phil Gates

Talk of war

The last day of a terrible year in the fell country – the thousands of little tragedies in the hills, the strangely deserted sheep pastures, the smoke from the burning pyres desecrating the lovely landscape, the fells out of bounds for much of the year, tourism sorely threatened and, after September, nothing but talk of vengeance and war.

I remember long months when mountain folk, denied the heights, had to trudge instead along traffic-congested roads. Memories of Morecambe promenade and the 'Struggle' from Ambleside to Kirkstone and back, come flooding in, as well as a few pleasant trips along neglected country lanes – especially Paddy Lane, high above Kendal, with its glorious Lakeland views from the shoulder of Benson Knott. Then, in late October, a return trip to a favourite prewar haunt, the beautiful Isle of Arran, spoiled by the often lovely autumn weather at its wettest worst.

Most clearly, I recall yesterday's Christmas tramp up and around the golf course behind my house. Here is one of the 'lungs of Kendal', where you can breathe mountain air after a short walk from the town streets, all a-glitter with the Christmas lights. There was a dusting of new snow on the Howgills and the High Street fells but hardly a speck on the Scafells and the Coniston hills, since the cold weather was coming in from the east. The ground was rock hard, the pools and puddles frozen over and the wind bitingly cold. There was nobody about and the low sun cast long shadows across the deserted greens. Just behind Gragareth, the top of Ingleborough peeped up and smiled down. I was sure 2002 would be a better year.

A Harry Griffin

The world on fire

ஜ October 2001 ௸

A big, fat harvest moon swings up above the hanging woods, through the wild smoke of night clouds. Nights are moody and quickening. Days are exhilarating, with thrashing winds, pelting rain and searingly bright flashes of sunlight.

There's nothing mellow about autumn. Morning mists send sensuous wraiths through trees, fingering the fields. Fruitfulness is light made flesh. Something turns, in the air and soil, coursing through the juices to the seed. Those fiery, orange-reds – the colour of Mars, the planet of war, like those devastating explosions constantly repeated on our television screens – are at the point of this turning.

Millions of leaves are turning, and the signs are that this will be one of the most spectacular flashes of autumn colour for many years. Hawthorns, brambles, wild cherry and field maples are catching fire, showing vivid flashes of scarlets and oranges.

Inside these leaves, the pigment anthocyanin, which is also responsible for reds and blues in flowers, is being released. Anthocyanin contains a protein that has fed and gained strength form the growing conditions of this year.

Perhaps the intensity of colour in flower, fruit and leaf has something to do with climate change, the effect of last winter and seasonal disruption too. Whatever, it certainly feels uplifting at a time when the world seems to have gone insane. Bright colours and dark deeds. Deadly rhetoric and simple pleasures. It almost seems sinful to enjoy the world around us. But then, these colours have a power we cannot deny. Terrible violence and great beauty can wear the same colours. War and autumn, the fires are lit.

Paul Evans

The bombers fly again

₲ NOVEMBER 2006 ℞

Thomas Hardy's poem, In Time of 'The Breaking of Nations', pictures 'a man harrowing clods' in the Wessex landscape, apparently untouched by international conflict. But now warplanes fly from RNAS Yeovilton, and the other day I heard from a reader who recalled a stick of incendiary bombs falling on her home in 1941, a few hundred yards from where I sit, and a German pilot coming down and being taken to the Templecombe maternity hospital a mile or so away. 'Poor man,' she writes, 'he had nothing to read, and we produced the only German book in the neighbourhood, an anthology of Schiller's poems.'

People gathered at the war memorials last week and, by coincidence, I had learned of two buildings in Castle Cary that mark a direct connection between the peacetime occupations of the surrounding dairy country and the first world war. One is Park Cottage up on the slopes south of the town, and the other is a substantial building of brick and stone in south Cary, formerly the cheese store of Mr Mackie, the cheese factor. In December 1914 a letter from one of the three young Mackie sons, all serving in the Somerset Light Infantry, dropped on the mat of Park Cottage, and others followed regularly from overseas throughout the war. They have been preserved and published in *Answering the Call*, edited by the writer's nephew, John HF Mackie. All three brothers survived the war. In September 1915, James Mackie writes from Port Blair in India: 'I am glad you have such a fine litter of pigs,' and goes on to comment on the price of eggs and butter at home. One letter refers to a cheese that has arrived in perfect condition after completing the last leg of its journey from the cool cheese store in a hot Indian train, and in March 1916 he writes of another, 'a real beauty, even better than the last one'.

John Vallins

A debt unpaid

ଚ୬ NOVEMBER 2005 ଚ୬

Alone, I pace the springy turf of a green path leading up from Llyn Tecwyn Isaf into the northern Rhinogydd. These are the most wild and strange hills in the whole mountainous land of Wales. Ifor Williams, in his standard work *Enwau Lleoedd*, (*Names of Places*), has the meaning as an elision of *yr hiniog* – the threshold – and I never come here without an encroaching sense of something otherworldly about them. Today, splashing on into the mist, the unremitting rain falling, I focus on the close particularities of place: the drop-beaded red blades of moor-grass; mist-wraiths' disorientating swirl; a ring-cairn alongside the track. Within this enclosed horizon there are soft mutterings of the wind of the sounds half-heard and the movement glimpsed only at the corner of an eye. And memories too – of a day long gone with my son Will, seven years old and clinging close in nervous apprehension of what might inhabit here, his mind full of story ...

The old way curves round above a morass to join the ancient trackway that climbs in from the south-west. A quick breeze roams in from that direction, lifts the skirts of the clouds and hustles them away. Suddenly, outlined on the crest of a bluff, Bryn Cader Faner stands stark and clear. Crown-like, stones pointing outwards, it has an intimate majesty perfectly in harmony with the cyclopean masonry of its setting. Four thousand years old, its artistry and mystery still impress. But less so than formerly, and from fewer angles. Soldiers on exercise in the second world war destroyed much of it. The desecrated stones still lie scattered about. The Ministry of Defence, in reparation, should carefully restore them. I wonder if it ever will?

Jim Perrin

Not forgotten

§⃝ June 2003 ⃝§

On a wet and windy day last winter I rode my bicycle up to the village and passed by the local cemetery. The simple and dignified graves of the Commonwealth War Graves Commission caught my eye, largely because of the way their design conflicted with the ornate stonework of Catholic burial. The inscriptions on the stones of six young RAF personnel, all killed on the same day, January 29 1943, suggested to me the crew of a Lancaster, short only of the pilot.

After I had written about this, it only took days for me to become very much better informed. Peter, writing from Hull, pointed me to the volume *RAF Bomber Command Losses, 1943*, and for Margaret, writing from London, I had clearly raised a personal agenda when she read my piece. Peter enclosed a photocopy, from which I learned that the Halifax of 158 Squadron had taken off from RAF Rufforth, near York, at 17.12 and came down near the coastal village of Plougasnou with the loss of the entire crew. The pilot has no known grave; the six gravestones describe and commemorate the necessary roles of a bomber crew on a mission to attack the submarine pens at Lorient, which had sent out so many of the Atlantic missions that sank thousands of tonnes of merchant shipping.

I was pleased also to find that local Breton historians writing for both the tourist market and for the record include this wartime drama with some rather foggy photos of the crash scene. Even the young lady in the tourist office, of a generation to regard the second world war as ancient history, was knowledgeable about the event and launched into a voluble account.

Colin Luckhurst

The highest memorial

ഉ NOVEMBER 2002 ෬

The day had started with heavy rain and grey mists drifting across the summit – much the same weather as on the day, 78 years ago, when the memorial tablet was dedicated. But later, the other day, the rain stopped, the clouds rolled away and the rocks began to steam in the bright November sunshine. This, a week ago, when the bands and television cameras were busy among the crowds at the Cenotaph, was the highest Remembrance Sunday in England – on the top of Great Gable, the favourite Lakeland summit of many mountain folk. Not so many people up there as in Whitehall but many hundreds of them, perhaps a thousand or so, all of whom had walked and scrambled up the long, stony climb to the summit.

This modern mass pilgrimage – Honister Pass blocked with parked cars – has become a public occasion of recent years: these fell tops now belong to the nation. But how many of the anoraked crowds were aware that the war memorial is not just the bronze tablet near the summit cairn but the freedom of the unchanging Wasdale hills for all people for all time?

The Fell and Rock Climbing Club purchased the summits of 12 fells, 1,184 acres in all, in 1924, as the memorial to their members killed in the first world war, and handed them over to the National Trust for safekeeping. Unsuccessful attempts had been made earlier to purchase Pillar Rock or Napes Needle as the memorial, until the club's far-sighted decision to go for all the high land on either side of Styhead Pass. And so every November the crowds arrive from all parts of the country – many just for the day out.

A Harry Griffin

Full circle

ᔕ MARCH 2003 ᙚ

The days around the vernal equinox have been terrible and beautiful. Terrible because of the war and perhaps the most beautiful of March days anyone can remember. Somehow this does not seem right: bombs and bullets, birds and butterflies. But life, death and rebirth are all around us and the smallest things seem to have great significance.

For me, this began a couple of days before the equinox, with a dead bird. Like a child's handful of moss, his body lay under the window. A goldcrest, Europe's smallest bird, his neck had snapped against the glass and now, as Druids say, his spirit belongs to the sun. The fiery-gold head plumage against the green feathers of his body made him the ideal symbolic sacrifice to spring. His vivid brightness shone even in death.

Although spring flowers are brilliant, some of the most remarkable colours are held in the wings of butterflies. After hibernation throughout the winter, their trance of death, many spring-emerging butterflies can look quite battered. But those fluttering about here have been in fantastic condition. The peacock butterflies, with their enigmatic eye-masks and sumptuous purple wings, are spectacular, but the most amazing are the commas. In the bright sunlight a comma finds a warm stick and lands with wings closed, silver-grey with mysterious marks. They flick open, sculpted, comma-cut wings of coppery orange with jet-black glyphs, flashing messages that can only be read beyond the eyes.

What does this say to us? There are moments when nature breaks into our world, often on the softest wings, even as the bombers fly to the monstrous acts we are fixated on.

Paul Evans

THE DIARISTS 1914–2006

Thomas Coward, dyer and bleacher, ornithologist
Arthur Nicholson, farmer and businessman
Basil de Selincourt, writer and critic
Helena Swanwick, journalist and suffragette
George Muller, naturalist
Arnold Boyd, army officer and naturalist
MA (Surrey) unidentified
Ronald Garnett, cotton manufacturer
Gwen McBryde, artist and farmer
John Adams, journalist and teacher
Ambrose Heath, food writer
BA (Oxfordshire) unknown
John Harrison, writer and bird artist
A Harry Griffin, climber and journalist
Bill Campbell, teacher

Colin Luckhurst, assistant education director, Open University tutor
and farmer
Veronica Heath, journalist and author
Paul Evans, writer, broadcaster and conservationist
Virginia Spiers, geographer with Ministry of Agriculture
Roger Redfern, teacher and writer
Sarah Poyntz, English teacher
John Vallins, headmaster of Chetham's School of Music, Manchester
Mark Cocker, author and environmentalist
Rev Graham Long, United Reformed Church minister, writer and
mollusc specialist
Phil Gates, senior lecturer in botany at Durham University
John Thompson, insurance underwriter
Audrey Insch, teacher and environmentalist
Jim Perrin, mountaineer and author
Richard Mabey, writer and environmentalist
Ray Collier, forester and writer
Derek Niemann, RSPB youth magazine editor
Tony Greenbank, climber and journalist

INDEX OF DIARY WRITERS

MA

Ronald Garnett

Roger Redfern
Country remedies for war, *June 1998,* 5
Target practice, *July 2005,* 22
Tank tracks, *August 1997,* 26
A mighty memorial, *November 2005,* 228

Sarah Poyntz
Guns, bombs and a sword, *February 2001,* 17
Seaweed medicine, *March 2004,* 86

John Vallins
Blind man's fort, *April 1999,* 16
Scramble, scramble, *October 2003,* 30
The old ways, *September 2002,* 36
A lost world, *June 1998,* 93
The bombers fly again, *November 2006,* 232

Mark Cocker
Out of bounds, *March 2000,* 24
A good war for redstarts, *April 2001,* 135

Rev Graham Long
Hidden in the forest, *May 2004,* 199
Moulded by war, *November 2005,* 226

Phil Gates
Wartime sweethearts, *January 2005,* 23
Picking the flowers, *September 1989,* 159
Pillbox in the brambles, *September 2001,* 229

SELECT BIBLIOGRAPHY

Ayerst, David *The Guardian Omnibus 1821-1971* Collins 1973

Boyd, Arnold *The Country Diary of a Cheshire Man* Collins 1946

Calder, Angus *The People's War: Britain, 1939-45* Jonathan Cape 1969

Challinor, Raymond *The Struggle for Hearts and Minds* Bewick Press 1995

Gilbert, Sir Martin *A History of the Twentieth Century: The Concise Edition* Harper Perennial 2002

Hennell, T *Change in the Farm* Cambridge University Press 1934

Kightly, Charles *Country Voices: Life and Lore in Farm and Village* Thames & Hudson 1984

Kitteringham, Jennie *Country Girls in 19th Century England* History Workshop 1973

Moreau, R E *The Departed Village* Oxford University Press 1968

Rackham, Oliver *The Illustrated History of the Countryside* Weidenfeld & Nicholson 1994

Scurr, Donald *Root and Branch* National Federation of Post Office and BT Pensioners 1999

Thompson, Flora *Lark Rise to Candleford* Oxford University Press 1945

Wainwright, Martin (Ed.) *A Gleaming Landscape: A Hundred Years of the Guardian's Country Diary* Arum Press 2006

Woodforde, John *The Truth About Cottages* Routledge & Kegan Paul 1969

AUTHOR'S BIOGRAPHY

Martin Wainwright is Northern editor of the *Guardian* and a regular broadcaster. He has edited two previous collections of Country Diaries and is author, most recently, of *The Guardian Book of April Fool's Day*, a guide to the *Coast to Coast Walk* (Guardian Books and Aurum Press) and *Wainwright – the Man who loved the Lakes*, a study of the fellwalker and writer Alfred Wainwright (BBC Books).